MAPS *of* PARADISE

MAPS *of* PARADISE

ALESSANDRO SCAFI

THE BRITISH LIBRARY

Incipe, parve puer, risu cognoscere matrem

(Virgil, Fourth Eclogue 60.4)

To Bibi, my late mother, who gave me life
and sketched its path on a map of paradise

Author's Note

I am grateful to my editors: Catherine Delano-Smith for her generous
and all-pervasive help; Catherine Bradley for challenging and improving
my arguments; and Mary Alice Lowenthal for her comments on the
text. My thanks to Bobby Birchall for the elegant design of this book, to
Sally Nichols for her picture research and to Teresa Monachino
for helping me with creative direction. I am also grateful to
Leon Conrad, Mariana Giovino, Alastair Hamilton, Christopher Ligota,
Antonio Panaino, Jonathan Rolls, Marta Scafi, Julian Smith-Newman,
Muhammad Isa Waley and Hanna Vorholt for their advice.

First published 2013 by
The British Library
96 Euston Road
London NW1 2DB

ISBN 978 0 7123 5709 8

British Library Cataloguing
in Publication Data
A catalogue record for this book is available from The British Library

Designed by Bobby Birchall
Printed in Hong Kong

p.1: *Iodocus Hondius,* Paradisus, *from Gerard Mercator and
Iodocus Hondius,* Atlas Minor *(Amsterdam: Iodocus Hondius, 1607; 1610).
Detail of Fig 72: the vignette with Adam and Eve's Fall.*

p.2: *The Catalan Estense world map, ?Majorca, c.1450–60. Modena, Biblioteca
Estense, C.G.A. 1. Detail of Fig 56: parts of Europe, Asia, and Africa.*

CONTENTS

CHAPTER 1

PARADISE NOWHERE AND ELSEWHERE

Bayazid said, 'paradise is of no worth to those who love'. Rabia had a related saying: 'First the neighbour, then the house'. That is, the neighbour, or God, is more important than the house, or paradise.

FARID UD-DIN ATTAR, IRAN,
TWELFTH CENTURY

BEYOND THE CLOUD OF THE PRESENT MOMENT

United States of America, 9 September 1971: an English musician releases an album whose first track is a three-minute song imbued with melody and poetry. War is escalating in Vietnam; nuclear weapons pose a serious threat to the earth's environment and humanity; authoritarian governments and big multinational businesses impose a fabric of exploitation and oppression everywhere. The message of the new song is a call for peace, a reminder that we are all one country, one world, one people.

The song, *Imagine* by John Lennon, soon becomes iconic, soaring to worldwide fame and commercial success. For some, it is still one of the greatest melodies of modern times. Through it, the Liverpudlian singer and songwriter urged his listeners to envisage '...all the people living life in peace' and challenged them to imagine, with him, a world without any other world: 'Imagine there's no heaven, It's easy if you try, No hell below us, Above us only sky'.

Is it possible to imagine a world where there are no other worlds? With no heaven or hell and with only the sky above? The history of religion shows that throughout the ages and in various places humankind has yearned for a timeless elsewhere. For several millennia human civilisations have borne witness to a deeply rooted longing, pressing against the boundaries of history and geography, moving in search of a beyond: a universal nostalgia for perfect bliss, remote either in time or in space. There have even been people who have maintained that there is nothing beyond the visible universe, and yet have nevertheless tried to open their own windows on to the horizon of some unattainable 'otherness'. All around the globe throughout human history and in the most varied of ways, people have longed for another world. They have *imagined* a perfect happiness existing somewhere at some time, as John Lennon did in his song of a world without religion and without the concepts of heaven and hell. Whatever the guise, secular or religious, a recurring trait across humanity has been to envisage perfect happiness at some past or future time, and/or in some remote place in the present.

In Hindu tradition, for example, original harmony and perfection, now lost, return to the world at the end of a series of cosmic cycles. Then, after the destruction of the universe, the earth will once again offer up its fruits spontaneously, and humankind will, no less spontaneously, follow the law and order of the cosmos. Hindu sources also refer to a mythical Mount Meru, located in the middle of the universe and surrounded by the cosmic ocean, on the peak of which is the paradise of Brahma, god of creation and of all supernatural beings. Tales of mountain islands inhabited by immortals, furnished with palaces of gold and where jewels grow on trees, are found also in Taoism and Buddhism. The ancient civilisations, such as those of the Chinese, the Sumerians, the Babylonians and Egyptians, all had their visions of other worlds. The Inuit of the Arctic lands, the Celts of central Europe, the peoples of South American forests and African deserts all have their 'paradises'. The Greeks and Romans conceived of a Golden Age and 'Islands of the Blessed'. As the perfect habitat for the first human couple, the Garden of Eden was a Hebrew tradition long before Christians adopted the Hebrew Bible as their Old Testament and closed their

Previous page: *Sultan Muhammad*, Muhammad's Ascent to Heaven, *from a miniature made to illustrate a copy of the poems of Nizami; Tabriz, Persia, c.1540. London, British Library, MS Or. 2265, fol.195r. Detail of Fig 11: the Prophet Muhammad ascending to heaven.*

New Testament with the promise of a final perfection, to be established by God at the end of human history.

However described, all these paradises embody the past, refer to an inaccessible present and anticipate the future. In Europe, the nineteenth-century German philosopher Arthur Schopenhauer drew attention to the way that the enchantment of distance reveals paradises which then evaporate like a mirage. Happiness, according to Schopenhauer, is always in the future or in the past, never the present, which he likened to a small dark cloud driven by the wind over a sunny plain: all before and all behind is bright light, only the cloud itself casts a deep shadow. Yet however gloomy the place, and however cloudy the season, humankind yearns for the brightness that went before and is promised to come, and continues to search for the light beyond the horizon.

THE VICISSITUDES OF A WORD

As far as we know, a term pointing to 'paradise' first emerged on the lips of the Medes, a powerful and, for us, enigmatic ancient tribe in the Middle East and central Asia. In the late second millennium BC – more or less at the time when, according to the Bible, Moses led the Israelites to their Promised Land and when, according to Homeric mythology, the city of Troy fell to Odysseus's ruse of the Wooden Horse – the Medes settled on the Iranian plateau. By the seventh century BC they had formed a political confederation that a century later was conquered by Cyrus the Great and transformed into the Persian Empire. The Medes are important to our story, as we speculate that a Median word, possibly *pari-daiza-*, passed to the Persians (but here pronounced as pari-daida-) to signify an enclosure. From *pari-*, meaning 'around', and *daiza-*, meaning 'a wall made of a malleable substance', such as clay (and derived from *diz-*, 'to mould' or 'to form'), in ancient Iran the word stood for something surrounded by a wall.

Words travel, and are liable to change their meaning along the way. The Persians conquered Babylon in 539 BC, and Babylonian documents dating from after the conquest contain the word *pardesu*, here referring to a vineyard. Clay tablets written between the sixth and the fifth centuries BC in Elamite, one of the official languages of the Persian administration, feature the word *partetas* (corresponding to a related Old Persian word, *pari-daida-*), indicating a storage place.

Shared historical events – such as the Graeco-Persian wars and the return of the Hebrew exiles to Judaea after the Babylonian captivity – as well as trade gave contemporary Hebrews and Greeks the word 'paradise' in their respective languages. Thus the Jewish prophet Nehemiah, who lived in the second half of the fifth century BC, and the unknown author of the *Song of Songs* (c.400 BC) used the Hebrew *pardes* to describe an orchard, a place in which to grow trees. *Paridaiza-* also appeared in ancient Greek as *parádeisos* [pron. parádêsos]. The word was used in this form by Xenophon, the fourth-century BC Greek soldier and historian.

As a matter of fact, we are left with no direct textual evidence of the early Median or Persian usage of the term: we only learn from the writings of Xenophon, a Greek familiar with the Persians, that in the ancient Persian empire the Median term *pari-daiza-* indicated a hunting park for the enjoyment of the elite, especially kings. The term has been hypothetically reconstructed from the spelling *pari-daêza-* attested in Avestan (the old Iranian language used in the *Avesta*, the Zoroastrian sacred text). The Persian *parádeisos*, then, pointed to a large, well watered field, containing trees, flowers and animals and enclosed by a wall. Here royals and aristocrats chased wild beasts for recreation and to keep fit for war.

The Empire founded in the sixth century BC by Cyrus the Great crumbled two centuries later with Alexander the Great's invasion of Persia, but some of its semantic legacy survived in Hellenistic and Roman Egypt, where *parádeisos* was used to indicate a pleasant garden or a royal park. The association of the word with divine perfection was first made when Ptolemy II Philadelphus, the third-century pharaoh of Hellenistic Egypt, had royal parks laid out around his palace on the model of the majestic Persian 'paradises'. Keen to enrich the great library in Alexandria and to incorporate its splendour into his court, the pharaoh ordered a group of Jewish scholars to translate the first five books of the Hebrew Bible (the Pentateuch) into Greek, at that time the *lingua franca* throughout the eastern Mediterranean.

From an apocryphal Greek document known as the *Letter of Aristeas* (which could have been composed any time between 200 BC and AD 33), we learn that our habit of referring to 'paradise' began with Ptolemy II's patronage of science and culture. According to the Aristeas tradition, six members from each of the 12 tribes of Israel (72 scholars in all) were summoned by the pharaoh from Jerusalem to Alexandria to make the translation of the Pentateuch for his library. After 72 days the 72 scholars had created a perfect rendering in Greek. Each scholar had worked independently, but divine inspiration ensured that each had produced an identical text.

The translation made in the third century BC for Ptolemy II is today known as the Septuagint, from *septuaginta* – a Latin allusion to the 70 scholars who completed it. (The term was later extended to designate the Greek version of the entire Old Testament adopted by Christians.) When they came to the Book of Genesis and the account about Adam and Eve, the Jewish scholars chose the words *parádeisos en Edem* ('paradise in Eden') for Genesis 2.8 and *parádeisos tês tryphês* ('paradise of delight') for Genesis 3.23. The Greek rendering of the Hebrew *gan eden* ('Garden of Eden') sought to convey the image of a royal park worthy of God's finest creation. No doubt the scholars imagined the perfect habitat given by God at the beginning of time to the first human couple to resemble an eastern royal 'paradise', created for pleasure (*eden* means delight') rather than hunting. The Greek *parádeisos*, however, went further than the Hebrew *gan* in specifically designating an enclosed park. Indeed the biblical Eden, a garden full of trees, irrigated by four rivers and guarded by an angel with a flaming sword, seemed to describe a true 'paradise' – an enclosed, pleasant and well watered grove similar to those enclosed parks enjoyed by Persian monarchs. Thus from indicating simply an enclosed space, the word came to convey the perfect primordial garden on earth.

Soon, however, the term 'paradise' experienced a further, more significant promotion. In the course of the second century BC, 'paradise' began to signify not

Fig 1 *'Paradise begins in Air Mauritius', 2001. The portrayal of paradise in advertising – the modern, secularised version of an old vision.*

just the primordial garden on earth, but also the blissful state of heaven, to be enjoyed by the righteous at the end of human history. How and why the extension of meaning came about is uncertain. It seems that Jews were beginning to take a special interest in their fate after death. They may have been inspired by Greek accounts of delightful abodes in the afterlife, at the edge of the earth in places endowed with a perfect climate and shaded by lush vegetation, reserved for a chosen few heroes or, as in the Orphic tradition, to larger groups of the righteous. Or they may have begun to employ the term 'paradise' to indicate the eternal condition of happiness and perfection they hoped to enjoy after death. In the lands of the eastern Mediterranean, a verdant garden stands out in stark contrast to the desolation of the desert in the same way that life is the opposite of death.

Early Christians embraced the concept, with the images of heaven as a paradisiacal garden, or *parádeisos*, appearing on many occasions in the New Testament. According to the Gospel of Luke (23.43, compiled in the first century AD), Christ on the cross promised 'paradise' to the good thief, meaning 'heaven'; in his second letter to the Corinthians (12.4) Paul maintained that a visionary flight to the third heaven had carried him into 'paradise'; and in the book of the Revelation of St John the Divine (2.7) Christians are promised a reward for faithfulness in a place called the 'paradise' of God. In later centuries, accounts of the visions of Christian martyrs, the verses of poets and the speculations of theologians describe the Christian world to come, the reward of the faithful, as a fragrant park, full of light and rich in all kind of plants and flowers – truly a 'paradise'. Sometimes this took the shape of a city, the Heavenly Jerusalem; though no longer a garden, it was still always referred to as 'paradise'. From the first centuries of Christianity, the term 'paradise', originally denoting an enclosed space or, more specifically, a royal game reserve suitable for walking in or for hunting, has been associated with the destination of the righteous in the life to come. Whether a garden or a city, and however mysteriously located in the beyond, the idea of a wonderful paradise awaiting the devout took root and has endured.

Nowadays, however, the word 'paradise' has been hijacked for commercial purposes by the tourist industry (Fig 1). In the Western world, advertisements for holidays promise 'paradise' to stressed city dwellers in the shape of some distant but welcoming luxurious natural environment – a place no more than a simple flight away, in which they can relax from the pressures and worries of the ordinary world. All that is needed to book a holiday in 'paradise' is some cash. Words do indeed travel, and their meaning changes along the way.

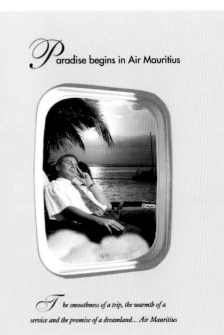

Paradise begins in Air Mauritius

The smoothness of a trip, the warmth of a service and the promise of a dreamland... Air Mauritius

ELUSIVE BUT EVERYWHERE

12 April 1961: for the first time ever, a human being leaves the earth's atmosphere and enters the void beyond, as Yuri Gagarin orbits the globe in a Soviet spacecraft. On his return, stepping out of the spaceship, he boasts that he has been in heaven, but that he has not seen God. That is not surprising: scientists and astronomers today do not seriously consider the possibility of finding either the creator of the world or a heavenly 'paradise' in outer space. Notwithstanding, countless people on earth persist in worshipping a deity who is somewhere up there in heaven.

It is 1520, and we are in the University of Salamanca, in western Spain. Professor Pedro Margalho, a Portuguese cosmographer educated in Paris, has published his *Physicae compendium*. In this learned treatise he compares medieval doctrines about earth and water, lands and seas, views on the ground and distances in the sky with the actual experience of contemporary Portuguese navigators, who are leading the great European voyages of exploration. Margalho is well versed in canon law, scholastic theology and natural philosophy, and has been closely following all recent advances in geographical knowledge. In his book, he wonders whether the Portuguese seafarers have encountered the earthly paradise as they are sailing all over the world.

In fact they had made no such discovery. They were not, of course, really looking for paradise; nobody assumed Eden was to be found just around the corner. Nevertheless,

Fig 2 (below) *Antonio Tempesta,* The Golden Age, *etching, Rome, 1599. London, British Museum.*

Fig 3 (above) *Cherubino Alberti, after Polydoro da Caravaggio,* Nymphs in the Garden of Hesperides picking the golden apples, *Rome, 1570–1615. London, British Museum.*

the widespread belief in Western Europe, one which the Portuguese sailors would have shared, was that the Edenic garden, once inhabited by Adam and Eve, existed somewhere in a remote but inaccessible corner of the planet. The existence of a paradise in some mysterious 'beyond' on earth was beyond question.

It now seems that the notion of a paradise, located neither on earth nor in the heavens, has always existed and is ubiquitous. 'Paradise' is an enduring word that has permeated the different cultures of the Mediterranean basin. As we have seen, it has travelled from Persia, Greece and Palestine to Christian Europe. From first evoking plain clay walls, the word passed on to an incomparable and unsurpassable association with a heavenly region. Now it features as a global concept in discussions of world civilisations. Historians of religion and anthropologists explore different expressions of 'paradise' in religions, past and present, all over the world. It is clearly not restricted to Judaism or Christianity, reflecting rather a fundamental human need to experience, in one form or another, a nostalgia for the blessed state we call 'paradisiacal'. However this nostalgia is named or whatever form it is given – a perfect joy experienced at the beginning of time, or one that awaits us at time's end, or that is hidden in a secluded place – the common thread is that paradise remains inaccessible to living people and that it is outside ordinary human time.

A PARADISE REMOTE IN TIME OR SPACE

Many cultural traditions tell us that a 'paradise' existed yesterday, during a marvellous Golden Age; that it will return tomorrow in the glory of a divine eternity, when the imperfect world comes to an end; or that 'paradise' is already here, on some mysterious island beyond the ocean or in some remote place that we cannot reach. The world's literature is rich in stories about times of peace, plenty and justice, and packed with accounts of secluded realms where fountains of immortality play and it is always spring. It would take endless time and unlimited space to account in detail for every human vision, individual or cultural, of a paradise out of time and space. Instead, we shall briefly explore the European classical tradition to make the point.

In the literature of ancient Greece and Rome lands of the blessed and ages of immeasurable happiness abound. Poets such as Hesiod and Ovid and philosophers such as Plato praised the perfection of a lost Golden Age, when Kronos, father of Zeus, ruled and when humans had no need to work, or to give birth; instead, they were gently 'shepherded' by divine personages (Fig 2). That was when, Plato tells us, God himself spoke directly to humans, trees and crops flourished in abundance, producing rich harvest without cultivation, and people spent the time roaming about in the open air unclothed, bathed in the benign climate (*Statesman*, 271e–272a). In his *Metamorphoses* Ovid sang of a time when there was no need for laws, judges or penalties as men and women did what was right of their own accord. Then the nations of the world lived harmoniously in leisure and peace, untroubled by fear or war, and there was only

Fig 4 (left) *Frederic Leighton,* The Garden of the Hesperides, *United Kingdom, c.1892. Liverpool, Lady Lever Art Gallery.*

everlasting spring, lush vegetation, peaceful breezes and rivers flowing with milk and nectar (I.89–112).

The notion of primordial perfection also had a spatial dimension, for some in Greece and Rome thought the Golden Age had survived on distant and elusive islands. Hesiod told how Kronos transferred his kingdom to the Elysian Fields (Figs 5 and 6, *Works and Days*, 170–175). Homer and Pindar praised the beauty of the Elysian Fields and the Islands of the Blessed that lay beyond the Ocean (*The Odyssey*, IV.563–68; *Olympian*, II.68–75). Apollodorus, Diodorus of Sicily, Hyginus and others wrote about the Garden of the Hesperides, another similarily blessed land. (Figs 3 and 4) Not everybody looked backwards to a Golden Age or tried to glimpse in the present a blessed island at the edge of space. Another tradition in classical times placed paradise in the future. In Virgil's *Fourth Eclogue*, for instance, the poet saluted the beginning of a new era of plenty, peace and justice that was soon to come about (5–10; 18–46).

Figs 5 and 6 (right, detail, and overleaf) *Sebastiano Conca, The Vision of Aeneas in the Elysian Fields, Italy, 1735–41. Sarasota, Florida, US, Bequest of John Ringling, 1936 collection of The John and Mable Ringling Museum of Art, the State Art Museum of Florida.*

PARADISE IN ISLAM

Both the word and concept of paradise passed from ancient Median into Arabic and thus, in due course, into Islam. The Arabic counterpart of 'paradise', however, *firdaws* (with the letter 'f' replacing 'p', missing from the Arabic alphabet), is only sparingly used. It generally refers exclusively to the highest level of paradise, destined for martyrs and prophets. For Muslims, paradise is a future garden in heaven, and the usual term in Islam is *jannah*, meaning 'garden'.

The everlasting bliss of paradise is related in the Qur'an and in the sayings attributed to the prophet Muhammad in sensual terms, but always with the qualification that such blessings are indescribable. The faithful are promised an afterlife of total pleasure in a place of cool shade and clear springs, wonderful food and unimaginable delights in the presence of the Omnipotent. Life in this garden of felicity and eternity will be enjoyed in uninterrupted peace and ardent love of God. Those who on earth trusted God's promises and carried out good deeds will forever rejoice with their spouses, family and friends as they glow with happiness. The blessed will be dressed in fine silks and heavy brocades, adorned with bracelets of gold, silver and pearls; they will recline on rich carpets or on raised thrones encrusted with precious stones, while being served delicious food in magnificent banquets by immortal youths. Both men and women will have whatever they wish for and will enjoy the company of pure and holy companions. Men will be greeted by the *houris*, devoted and loving virgins of perpetual freshness, with large lustruous eyes that resemble pearls in their perfect beauty. Women will be restored young and beautiful; they will be reunited with their husbands and children, or provided by God with heavenly husbands who will delight their hearts. All sorrow and weariness will be lifted, all misery and hardship forgotten. Rivers of delicious wine, incorruptible water, unchanging milk and pure honey will flow around the blessed.

Such is the literal description. From early times, though, many Muslims have dwelt on the spiritual meanings that lie below the surface of the words of the Holy Qur'an. Avicenna, for example, a learned man of great faith who lived in Persia around AD 1000, understood the heavenly paradise as an intellectual vision of God and a veiled revelation of divine treasures.

Fig 7 (opposite) *Qur'an, Sura 1,* al-Fatihah *('The Opening'), Malay Peninsula, east coast, nineteenth century. London, British Library, Or. MS 15227, fol.3v.*

Fig 8 (right) *Qur'an, Sura 37,* al-Saffat *('The Ranked Fliers'), Persia, 1036. London, British Library, Add. MS 7214, fol.52v. Detail: the first 12 lines.*

Visual Prelude
A Luminous Ascension

The holiest place in Islam is the Kaaba in Mecca. At the easternmost corner of the building lies the Black Stone, believed to have been placed there by Abraham and his son Ishmael. The prophet Muhammad once kissed the stone and so do Muslim pilgrims (Fig 9). White when it fell to earth at the beginning of time, the stone turned black because of human sin, yet its message to the faithful tells of darkness leading to light and of the transcendence of evil. For it was at this sacred spot that the Prophet Muhammad met the archangel Gabriel who took him on a miraculous journey – first to Jerusalem (known as the *isra* or 'night journey') and then from Jerusalem to the seven levels of heaven in turn (known as the *miraj* or 'ladder').

The *miraj* was portrayed around 1540 by one of the greatest sixteenth-century Persian painters, Sultan Muhammad. He was the leading artist of the Turkoman school that flourished in Western Iran at that time. The miniature, considered to be his masterpiece, was part of a sequence created to illustrate a copy of a classical Persian work, the

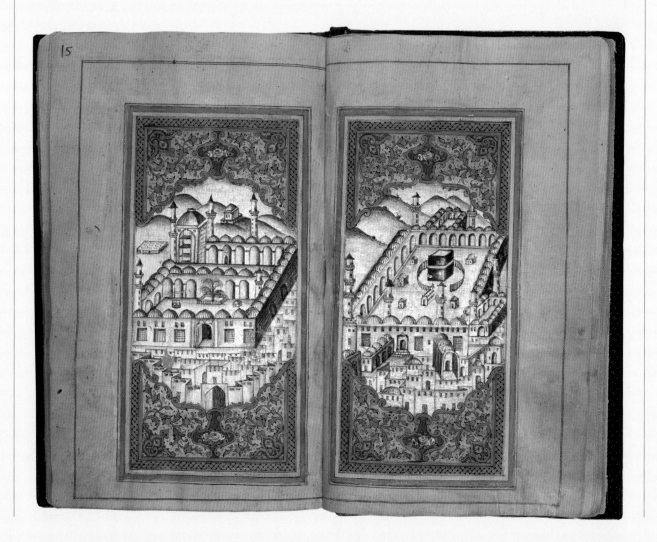

Khamsa ('Quintet', comprising one didactic text and four romances), by the twelfth-century poet Nizami (Fig 11).

Sultan Muhammad's manuscript illumination turned out to be a luminous image. The Prophet Muhammad is depicted ascending to paradise mounted on his steed *Buraq* ('lightning'). The human-headed horse had come down from heaven to transport him first from Mecca to Jerusalem, almost 800 miles, and then from Jerusalem to paradise, a distance known only to God, and back to Mecca – all in a single night. The Prophet is represented with his face covered, surrounded by angels and engulfed by sacred fire. *Buraq* is shown with a human head and the rump of a horse, while his tail and hoofs are like those of a camel. The brief and mysterious allusion in the Qur'an (Sura 17) to that memorable night was early embellished by a wealth of detail. From those supplementary writings about the life of the Prophet we learn that the extraordinary heavenly creature ridden by Muhammad had an emerald saddle, pearl reins and turquoise stirrups. When Sultan Muhammad embarked on his illumination he painted each figure in brilliant, vivid, almost violent colours, staging them with dynamic verve against a heaven packed with billowing clouds and flying angels.

Paradise itself is not depicted in Sultan Muhammad's painting. In the tradition of Islamic manuscript illumination relating to the *miraj*, only the Prophet's journey to and from heaven is represented; the viewer is given no direct glimpse into paradise, since the *miraj* is the Prophet's experience of transcending in his body the physical world. In Mecca the journey is re-enacted by the pilgrims undertaking the *hajj* (the pilgrimage) as a stage of their own journey towards paradise. The Kaaba, with the Black Stone within, is draped in black, and as they move towards the dark point each pilgrim is robed in white. The Kaaba is circumambulated seven times, in an anti-clockwise direction. Should the density of the crowds prevent pilgrims from reaching, and kissing, the Black Stone, they may point to it on each circuit. The goal of this ritual is to lead the faithful to paradise, a feast of light that the Prophet of Islam has reached through the darkest of nights. In the same way, the believer progresses through darkness into light.

Fig 9 (opposite) *Depiction of the Holy City of Mecca, from Muhammad ibn Sulayaman al-Jazuli*, Dala'il al-khayrat *('Guide to Goodness'), India, nineteenth century. London, British Library, MS Or. 16211, fol.15r.*

Fig 10 (right) *Detail of a fifteenth-century pilgrimage certificate, origin unknown, 1432–3. London, British Library, Add. MS 27566.*

Bibliographic Essay

◆

John Lennon's *Imagine* is the opening track of the homonymous album released in the United States and the United Kingdom on 9 September and 8 October 1971 respectively; it was reissued several times after the musician's death in 1980. *Imagine* was released as a single in the UK in 1975 and re-released several times subsequently.

Arthur Schopenhauer's remarks about paradise always being elsewhere are in *Die Welt als Wille und Vorstellung*, 3rd edn, 2 vols (Leipzig: Brockhaus, 1859), II, p.655; Richard B. Haldane and John Kemp, trans., *The World as Will and Idea*, 3 vols (London: Trübner, 1883-6), III (1886), p.383.

On the history of the term 'paradise' see Jan N. Bremmer, 'Paradise: From Persia, via Greece, into the Septuagint', in Gerard P. Luttikhuizen, ed., *Paradise Interpreted: Interpretations of Biblical Paradise: Judaism and Christianity* (Leiden–Boston, MA: Brill, 1999), pp.1–20; Bremmer, 'The Birth of Paradise: to Early Christianity via Greece, Persia and Israel', and Antonio Panaino, 'Around, Inside and Beyond the Walls: Names, Ideas and Images of *Paradise* in Pre-Islamic Iran', in Alessandro Scafi, ed., *The Cosmography of Paradise* (London–Turin: The Warburg Institute-Aragno, forthcoming). Pedro Margalho, *Phisices compendium* (Salamanca: 1520), fols.3r–6r, is quoted by Luis de Matos, *L'Expansion portugaise dans la litterature latine de la Renaissance* (Lisbon: Fundaçâo Calouste Gulbenkian, 1991), p.427.

Many books have been published to offer a general survey on world visions of paradise: see, for example, Pierre-Antoine Bernheim e Guy Stavridès, *Paradis, Paradis* (Paris: Plon, 1991).

On early Jewish and Christian ideas about paradise see Markus Bockmuehl and Guy G. Stroumsa, eds., *Paradise in Antiquity: Jewish and Christian Views* (Cambridge: Cambridge University Press, 2010) and Luttikhuizen, ed., *Paradise Interpreted*.

On Islamic paradise I have made use of 'Abdullah 'Abdurrahman Al-Shimemeri, ed., *Descriptions of Paradise from the Qur'aan and Hadeeth*, (Jeddah, Saudi Arabia: Abul-Qasim, 1994). See also Shemuel Tamari, *Iconotextual Studies in the Muslim Vision of Paradise* (Wiesbaden–Ramat-Gan: Harrassowitz–Bar-Ilan University, 1999); Sheila S. Blair and Jonathan M. Bloom, eds., *Images of Paradise in Islamic Art* (Hanover, NH: Hood Museum of Art, Dartmouth College, 1991); Aziz Azmah, 'Rhetoric for the Senses: A Consideration of Muslim Paradise Narratives', *Journal of Arabic Literature*, 26/3 (1995), pp.215–31; Muhammad A. Haalem, 'Life and beyond in the Qur'an', in Dan Cohn-Sherbok and Christopher Lewis, eds., *Beyond Death: Theological and Philosophical Reflections on Life after Death* (Palgrave Macmillan, 1995), pp.66–79; William A. Bijlefeld, 'Eschatology: Some Muslim and Christian Data', *Islam and Christian Muslim Relations*, 15/1 (2004), pp.35–54. On Sultan Muhammad see Stuart Cary Welch, *Persian Painting: Five Royal Safavid Manuscripts of the Sixteenth Century* (New York: Braziller, 1976). On the tradition about the *miraj*, a good bibliography is in Jamel Eddine Bencheikh, *Le Voyage nocturne de Mahomet* (Paris: Imprimerie Nationale, 1988), pp.291–300.

Fig 11 *Sultan Muhammad, Muhammad's* Ascent to Heaven, *from a miniature made to illustrate a copy of the poems of Nizami; Tabriz, Persia, c.1540. London, British Library MS Or. 2265, fol.195r.*

CHAPTER 2

MAPPING THE TERRITORY

*In that empire, the art of cartography attained such perfection that
a map of a single province occupied the entirety of a city, and the map of the
empire the entirety of a province. In time, those unconscionable maps no longer
satisfied, and the cartographer guilds struck a map of the empire whose size was
that of the empire, and which coincided point for point with it. The following
generations, who were not so fond of the study of cartography as their forebears
had been, saw that that vast map was useless, and not without some pitilessness
was it that they delivered it up to the inclemencies of sun and winters.
In the deserts of the west, still today, there are tattered ruins of the map,
inhabited by animals and beggars; in all the land there is no other
relic of the disciplines of geography.*

JORGE LUIS BORGES,
DEL RIGOR EN LA CIENCIA
('ON EXACTITUDE IN SCIENCE'), 1946,
ANDREW HURLEY, TRANS.

In Sanskrit Punyashila Dawadi's first name means 'one of virtuous character'. And appropriately Punyshila, who comes from Katmandu, was one of those who told the international magazine *Colors* how she envisioned heaven: 'In heaven people don't have to hang on to the doors of buses to get to college on time'. *Colors*' special issue on 'Heaven', published in the autumn of 1995, included a wide range of personal opinions (Fig 12). The editors acknowledged that heaven is, as they put it, 'a major selling point in the marketing of most religions'. At the same time they claimed that, in addition to all the official views on paradise, the ideas of individuals (which must total several billions) are no less important. So they asked people to share their views of what they thought paradise might be like.

Responses poured in. Kris Hamamoto from New York declared that 'in heaven the subway stations smell like ice cream', while for a Mexican lady, Bianca Hinojosa Gonzales, 'heaven on earth is feeling the wind on my face'. Others had different ideas,

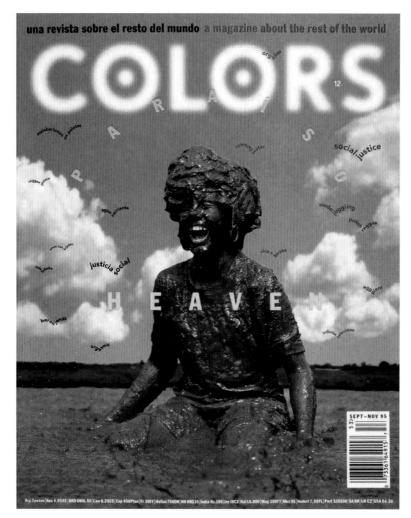

Previous page: *Giovanni Leardo, Mapa Mondi. Figura Mondi, Venice, 1442. Verona, Biblioteca Civica, MS 3119, unfoliated. Detail of Fig 15: the map of the world.*

Fig 12 (left) *Cover of* Colors *no.12 (September 1995).*

conceiving heaven as 'a huge library' (Cesar Ochoa Diez, Barcelona); a 'big white hole filled with stars, mountains, trees – and they're all white' (Karim Hussein, Cairo); 'the inner life of my handbag' (Sandra Prill, Hamburg); 'a cherry-red Porsche with Claudia Schiffer in the passenger seat' (Toby Hockin, Surrey, UK); 'when I see my last grand-daughter get married and start having children' (Suha Dabach, Dir-el-Assad, Israel).

The desire for a personal heaven tailored to supply what is missing from life on earth seems natural, in spite of the Buddha's insight that only by extinguishing desire may a person reach heaven. But *Colors*' innovative coverage of the myriad ways each individual in the human mass imagines his or her private heaven points up the seemingly unlimited number of ways of envisioning a perfect human state of wellbeing. Of course, these ways reflect significantly different viewpoints and depend on various cultural conditionings. Stressed-out Westerners may search for paradise on an exotic island isolated in a remote ocean, as advertised by the tourist industry. For the islander confined to such a remote, ocean-bound point, however, it may be the global crossroads of a big city that offers a paradise full of unfamiliar thrills and new opportunities. In the heat of a Middle Eastern desert, paradise takes the form of a shady and well watered garden; but for the Inuit peoples paradise is a place rich in seal meat and berries, somewhere it is possible to hunt without too great an effort.

How can we make sense of all the ancient traditions and modern secular motifs and their intermingling and overlapping? One way is to see paradise as a metaphor for a state of mind, and as both an actual condition and a symbol. This interpretation is common, in fact, to all manifestations in which paradise stands, on the one hand, for nostalgia for a lost primordial condition, a hope for the future or a yearning for a distant island and, on the other, for a spiritual dimension that is open to one and all at all times and in all places. Thus for Buddhists Nirvana is a perfect state of mind, achieved by controlling the baser side of self and through union with the Supreme Being. For Christians the image of a physical garden of paradise also represents the flourishing of the internal, spiritual aspect of humanity. What all religious authorities and writers, wherever they have been in the world and whatever their faith, have appreciated (and continue to do) is that try as they might to unveil the secrets of paradise, it is impossible to do full justice to the mystery. It is easy to feel lost in such a jungle of visions and beliefs. We need a map or guide to help us follow the trail.

One guide we can take is the first century BC Greek historian Diodorus of Sicily. He spent 30 years travelling widely and researching his monumental history of mankind, the *Bibliotheca historica*. In the end, though, Diodorus was driven to acknowledge that the writing (or telling) of history is unnatural. The historian, he pointed out, cannot describe simultaneously the many events that happened simultaneously, nor can words be arranged in the multiple and intricately interconnecting sequences that constitute life as it happens. To write a record, the historian has to construct a narrative. This means he has first to select what he thinks are the most important events of his story and then arrange them in succession. As a consequence the historian's viewpoint is always subjective and manipulative. Diodorus assured his readers that such distortion is inevitable and unavoidable, and that it should thus be regarded as a necessary condition of historical writing (*Bibliotheca historica*, X.20.43.7).

The ambition to attempt to record a complete series of contemporary events, to create an authentic history, is surely as foolish as impossible. Likewise it is impossible to map the fullness of geographical space, as the Argentinean author Jorge Luis Borges demonstrated 2,000 years after Diodorus. In Borges' famous short story about the relationship of map and territory, the writer imagines an ancient empire where a group of cartographers conceive a plan: to draw a topographical map on the scale of 1:1 of all the empire's lands, showing its towns and cities and every detail of the landscape – mountain ranges, islands, rivers and lakes (*Del rigor en la ciencia*, 'On Exactitude in Science', 1946). Of course the project was ridiculous. It was not only difficult to achieve, but the resultant map was of no use to anyone. The zealous imperial mapmakers' descendants did not know what to do with an awkwardly vast map that was impossible to handle. So the torn and worn map was abandoned, left to lie on the desolate desert sands, where its fragments were occasionally used for shelter by wild beasts and the homeless.

No history can ever offer a truly comprehensive account of the events it describes. Nor can any map ever be identical with the territory it portrays. Any serious attempt to map the historical process or the geographical landscape in all completeness would be madness. Yet we still need and use maps, and write and read histories. Even if some reality is lost from the historical account or the geographical map through selection, something is gained at the same time from both the history and the map. The jungle of visions and beliefs about paradise may be confusing, but it is possible to map a way out. To help us follow that trail, maps of paradise come to our assistance.

MAPS OF PARADISE

Christians have been drawing maps representing paradise for the last two millennia. They all concern a quite specific paradise: that of the Garden of Eden as described in the Book of Genesis, with which the Bible begins the Judaeo-Christian account of human history. Genesis was probably written down in the ninth or tenth century BC, but it must have incorporated a wealth of oral tradition handed down across possibly thousands of generations. The book tells how God planted a special place on earth as a home for the first human couple. It was an enchanting garden, into which Adam and Eve were placed by their Creator to live in a blissful state of total perfection. This was the earthly paradise. It marks the beginning of human time, just as the heavenly paradise (or Heavenly Jerusalem), described in Revelation, the final book of the Christian Bible, stands for its end. Both of these paradises (which border the space–time continuum of human history at either end) can be seen decorating a page of a fifteenth-century manuscript of Augustine's *City of God* (Fig 13). Here the primordial Garden of Eden is sited in the distance on the map in the centre; above it radiates the Heavenly Jerusalem coming down to earth in its full glory, with Christ bathed in light and surrounded by angelic choirs and precious stones. The scenes on

Fig 13 *Illuminated page from a manuscript of Augustine's* De civitate Dei, *Île de France or Normandy, c.1473–80. Mâcon, Bibliothèque Municipale, MS Franç. 2, fol.19r.*

the map portray some of the early events in human history after the Fall as recounted in the Book of Genesis.

Medieval and later mapmakers took up the challenge to locate the mysterious garden of Adam and Eve cartographically on earth. Their resulting maps now offer us a valuable point of entry for tracing – out of the tangle of contradicting notions and different traditions about paradise all over the world and throughout the centuries – a reliable history of attempts to reveal heaven on earth. These are the maps that can provide our own road maps, and that facilitate our telling of the story.

The following chapters are thus a review of the mapping of the biblical earthly paradise or Garden of Eden (the terms are used interchangeably). It is a history in itself, as it charts the way in which Eden was depicted on maps from the eighth to the twenty-first century. The beauty of many of the maps we shall encounter is no accident; their colour and charm reflect the profundity of belief underlying the mapping process. Beauty apart, however, our story is an important element (and a fascinating expression) of the West's intellectual history, not least because of the inherent paradox of mapping the unmappable. The vision with which we engage is the most alluring: it is the dream of perfect humanity displayed cartographically.

The Old Testament Book of Genesis is common to Christians and Jews, and one might expect to start the story of mapping the earthly paradise with reference to the Hebrew tradition. However, apart from the problem of divergent traditions concerning its location, it seems that the rabbis of pre-Christian times were more interested in other issues raised by the Genesis account of the Garden of Eden, such as the relationship between man and woman and the nature of the authority that humankind has over the earth. Moreover, whatever may have been drawn, no corpus of pre-Christian Jewish maps has survived.

As will be explained in the next chapter, Christian interest in the location and mapping of the earthly paradise was sparked mainly in the fifth century AD by St Augustine's literal interpretation of the Genesis narrative. Moreover, this rather special cartographic impulse tended to be restricted to Latin Christian Europe. Eastern Christians preferred a symbolic reading of the paradise narrative and turned to other theologians, such as Basil the Great, Gregory of Nyssa and John Chrysostom, rather than Augustine, as their spiritual and exegetical Fathers, for example. Islamic paradise, expressed in human and sensual terms, was nevertheless believed to be in heaven, too distant from the geographical world to be mapped together with the regions of the earth. Islamic maps of the world only occasionally feature the mythical Mountain of Qaf that encircles the ocean surrounding the earth. The Garden of Eden is not found, then, on Islamic maps (Arab, Persian and Turkish). Just occasionally the eastern region where Adam and Eve were believed to have fallen (from heaven to the earth) after their sin is marked.

The belief in an earthly paradise, and the persistent attempts to show its location on maps, highlight a fundamental Western tension – the desire to have heaven on earth. Paradise is found in almost every form of cultural expression – poetry, visual art, literary and philosophical writing – but the enterprise of depicting paradise on a map of the world, or part of the world, has always presented the mapmaker with a major intellectual challenge. Today, when maps are made with the help of satellite and radar electronics that mirror unerringly almost every centimetre of the globe, there is no room for representations of the earthly paradise. We should bear in mind how greatly the assumptions, and techniques that govern modern cartography differ from those of medieval and early modern Europe if we are to visit the 'foreign country' of our past and understand the intellectual conditions that allowed a theological concept to be mapped. As Oscar Wilde pointed out, a map of the world that does not include some other world of a different kind is not even worth glancing at.

Fig 14 Detail of Fig 13. Augustine is responding to a group of philosophers by reasserting the uniqueness of the creation of the world by God. The point is confirmed by another figure of Augustine in the enlarged letter at the beginning of the text.

Visual Interlude
Paradise on the Leardo Map

◆

One day in 1442 the Venetian cartographer Giovanni Leardo laid down his pen, having signed and dated the map he had just completed (Fig 15). It was a masterpiece, blending text and image into a portrait of the earth. In a text below the map proper, he identified the three concentric circles that surround the earth. The innermost indicated the 12 months of the year, the second contained the 12 signs of the zodiac and the outermost gave the dates for Easter for the next 100 years or so. Leardo knew that by reckoning of the date of Easter, which had to fall on the first Sunday following the first full moon after the spring equinox, human time, religious truths and heavenly rhythms would be reconciled. On the circle with the zodiac, the top of the map coincides with the passage from Pisces to Aries – the constellation believed to have been in the ascendant when God created the world, Mary conceived the Saviour and Christ was resurrected from the dead.

Once it is realised that east, marked by a decorative cross, is at the top of the map, the outlines of the Mediterranean Sea and Europe are readily recognised, for Leardo delineated them with great accuracy. As was not unusual in late medieval and early Renaissance times, he must have taken his outlines from a nautical chart, a quite different type of map used in contemporary navigation. For other aspects of world geography, he followed the biblical text. For example, he emphasised the centrality of Jerusalem by placing the city at the intersection of the two lines which divide the map into four quarters.

On Leardo's map, the east–west (vertical) line cuts across the Indian Ocean, crosses the Persian Gulf, reaches the Mediterranean just south of Cyprus and touches the coasts of Africa at Tunis. Passing through Spain and Portugal, it terminates in the *Mar de Spagnia*, the Sea of Spain. The horizontal line links north and south. It passes first through the inscription *Dixerto dexabitado per fredo* ('desert uninhabited because of the cold'), then cuts across the River Don and the Black Sea, the Red Sea, Ethiopia and the 'Land of the Pharaohs' before reaching another inscription which announces *Dixerto dexabitado per chaldo e per serpenti* ('desert uninhabited because of heat and snakes'). The two deserts on the map – one in the north and one in the south, both uninhabitable because of extremes of temperature – coincide with the two solstices (December and June) indicated on the encircling calendar.

Leardo's map depicts the whole of the habitable world as it was known in the mid-fifteenth century. Fully aware that the earth is a sphere, but faced with the problem of representing a globe on a flat surface, Leardo could show on his circular map only the known and inhabited portion of the earth – the northern hemisphere. Accordingly his world stretches from the Far East to the Atlantic, and from the dark and cold northern deserts, corresponding to the Arctic Circle, to the torrid regions of Africa. It is still a world of Asia, Africa and Europe; it would be another 50 years before Christopher Columbus added a New World to the map of the world.

Leardo's map is highly detailed, showing mountain ranges, islands, rivers and lakes. Vignettes of castles, walled towns and churches represent regions as well as towns and cities. In Europe places are located accurately, but in Asia the entire Indian

Fig 15 *Giovanni Leardo,* Mapa Mondi; Figura Mondi, *Venice, 1442. Verona, Biblioteca Civica, MS 3119, unfoliated.*

PISIS
MARZO
ARIES
APRILE
TAURUS
MAZO
GEMINI
ZUGNIO
CANCER
LUIO
LEO
AVOSTO
VIRGO
SETENBRO
LIBRA
OTUBRIO
NOVENBRIO
SAGITARIO
DEZENBRIO
ZENARO
AQUARIO
FREVARO

subcontinent is missing. Rather unexpectedly, Africa is divided into two parts, a northern and a southern part. The seas are coloured blue, except for the Red Sea, which is suitably red. Here and there little notes tell us that, for example, on some islands in the Indian Ocean pepper and other spices are found, and that in the middle of Asia there are people who eat human flesh.

By the standards of his time, Leardo was an accurate mapmaker, and he had evidently taken considerable pains over the layout of the Mediterranean and Europe. Several inscriptions in Asia include information taken from travel accounts of relatively recent and trustworthy explorers, such as Marco Polo. Place names in Africa and the Far East came from Ptolemy's *Geography*, which had been translated into Latin earlier in the fifteenth century. Care had also been taken over the calendar. So we may be surprised to

find the earthly paradise also depicted on Leardo's map of the world (Fig 16). A vignette placed on the map close to India portrays an exceptionally beautiful city, with a tall column in the centre surrounded by splendid buildings, clearly labelled in red ink, and in fifteenth-century Venetian vernacular, *paradixo teresto*.

To the modern mind the presence of the Garden of Eden on a map of the world throws into doubt the seriousness of Leardo's cartographical enterprise. How could a careful cartographer, who used up-to-date navigational charts as his base map, include on a modern map of the world something as intangible as the earthly paradise, a place described in the Bible as inaccessible to man? Why, if he had to show it, did he choose to place it near India? Were his contemporaries expected to believe that Leardo's *paradixo teresto* was really in that particular place?

Bibliographic Essay

———— ◆ ————

Jorge Luis Borges first published his famous short story about map and territory under a pseudonym in *Los Anales de Buenos Aires* in 1946 (1/3). Later in 1946 the story was included in his *Historia Universal de la Infamia* ('A Universal History of Infamy'). Andrew Hurley's English translation (quoted above) was published in Borges, *Collected Fictions* (New York: Penguin, 1998), p.325.

Colors is a quarterly magazine created by Tibor Kalman and Oliviero Toscani in 1991 and published in Northern Italy by the fashion brand *Benetton* in three editions: English plus French, Italian and Spanish. The September/November 1995 issue had 'heaven' as a main theme, covered from an international perspective and with an innovative design inspired by modern advertising.

Luciano Canfora, author of *Totalità e selezione nella storiografia classica* (Bari: Laterza, 1972), quotes the Diodorus of Sicily passage in his 'Aspetti e problemi della narrazione storica' in *Il mondo contemporaneo*, X (Florence: La Nuova Italia, 1983), pp.861–80; he also provides a useful bibliography on methodological issues in history writing. On the claims of Greek and Roman historians to write authoritative accounts see John Marincola, *Authority and Tradition in Ancient Historiography* (Cambridge: Cambridge University Press, 1997). Emilie Savage Smith, 'In Medieval Islamic Cosmography, Where is Paradise?' in

Alessandro Scafi, ed., *The Cosmography of Paradise* (London–Turin: The Warburg Institute–Aragno, forthcoming), discusses why Islamic maps do not feature paradise on earth.

Oscar Wilde's quotation ('A map of the world that does not include utopia is not even worth glancing at') comes from his *The Soul of Man under Socialism*, orig. published in 1891, in *The Artist as Critic*, Richard Ellmann, ed., (New York: Random House, 1969), p.269.

On the various Leardo maps see Giovanni Dal Lago, 'Giovanni Leardo, *Mapa Mondi*', in Guglielmo Cavallo, ed., *Due mondi a confronto 1492–1728. Cristoforo Colombo e l'apertura degli spazi*, 2 vols (Rome: Istituto poligrafico e Zecca dello Stato–Libreria dello Stato, 1992), I, pp.159–162, with bibliography; Pompeo Durazzo, *Il planisfero di Giovanni Leardo* (Mantua: Eredi Segna, 1885); John K. Wright, *The Leardo Map of the World, 1452 or 1453, in the Collections of the American Geographical Society* (New York: American Geographical Society, 1928); Evelyn Edson, 'World Maps and Easter Tables: Medieval Maps in Context', *Imago Mundi*, 48 (1996), pp.25–42.

For this and the following chapters, the interested reader will find more material and full bibliographical references in my *Mapping Paradise: A History of Heaven on Earth* (London–Chicago: British Library–University of Chicago Press, 2006).

Fig 16 *Detail of Fig 15: the earthly paradise.*

CHAPTER 3

MAPPING THE BIBLE

St Amaro had a fixed idea that wouldn't leave him in peace: at least once in his life he wanted to look upon the Garden of Eden in which Adam and Eve had lived at the beginning of time. In his books he had read that the paradise from which Adam was driven was a splendid garden, a garden which, even if it was now uninhabited, could still be found somewhere on earth. According to these books, the earthly paradise was in the first region of Asia.

Finally, one day he took to the sea, spreading the sails to the winds and letting them carry him. At long last, he landed on the shores of a delightful island and came within sight of a marvellous palace, studded and resplendent with precious stones. Everything shone with an incomparable light. At the gate stood a youth with radiant features, a sword in his hand. With his heart in his mouth, Saint Amaro approached the magnificent portal, asking the gatekeeper permission to enter. After man's original sin, however, no mortal was granted the right to re-enter Eden, and for this reason the angel denied the holy traveller the permission to proceed. Amaro had to be satisfied with gazing at the garden from the threshold. From there, however, he was still able to discern splendid meadows covered with flowers and watered by limpid, luminous streams.

FROM A SIXTEENTH-CENTURY
SPANISH LEGEND

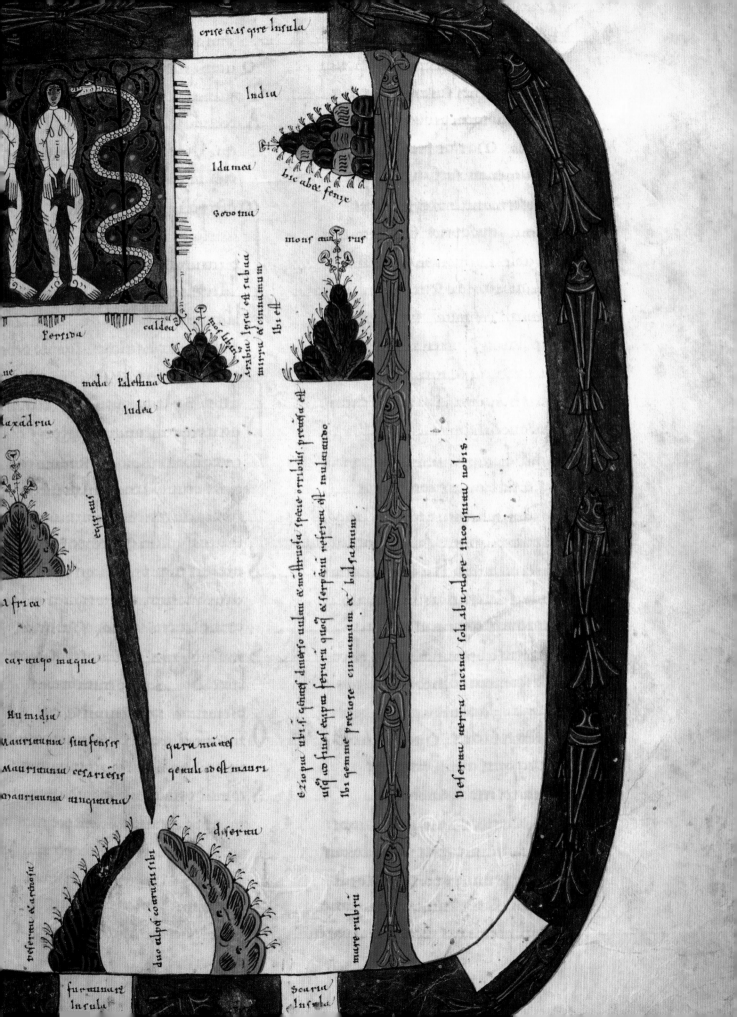

crise etas qre insula

India

Idumea

Sodoma

hic abet fenix

mons cinnamr rus

araba ipra et sabaa
mirra et cinnamum
ihi est

mos libani

Persida

Caldea

meda   Palestina

Iudea

Alaxandria

egiptus

africa

carrago magna

Numidia

Mauritania sirifensis

Mauritania cesariensis

Mauritania tingitania

garamantes

getuli id est mauri

diserta

deferta et arenosa

duo alpes conucris ibi

Etiopia ubi f. genes dinerse untur ac monstruosa spene orribiles. precisa est
usq ad fines egipti ferrua quoq et serpentiu referta est. Multaquibo
ibi gemme preciose cinnamum et balsamum.

deferta terra uicina soli aburore inco gnita nobis.

mare rubru

The Bible opens with the story of the creation of the world by God. The first chapter of the Book of Genesis records how God completed his work in six days. On the first day God created light, separating it from darkness. On the second day he formed the firmament, or expanse of the sky. On the third day he created the land, with its plants and trees, distinguishing it from the sea (Fig 17). On the fourth day the stars, the sun and the moon were created, and on the fifth day the fish and the birds. Man was fashioned on the sixth day, together with the animals. Finally, on the seventh day, as described at the beginning of the second chapter, God finished his work and rested, creating nothing new thereafter.

Later in the second chapter of Genesis, God is once again described fashioning a human being, a man into whose nostrils he breathes life (Fig 18). It is in this second account that we read how God created a garden for the nurturing of this human creature (verse 8), and how he ordained that all kinds of trees should grow there,

Previous page: *Map of the world, from a manuscript of Beatus of Liébana's* In Apocalypsin, *Monastery of Santo Domingo de Silos, 1106 (detail of Fig 27). London, British Library, Add. MS 11695, fol.40r.*

Fig 17 (left) Creation, Third Day, *from Peter Comestor,* Historia scholastica *(orig. compiled twelfth century), Bohemia, early fifteenth century. Vatican City, Biblioteca Apostolica Vaticana, Vat. Lat. 5697, fol.7r.*

Fig 18 (right) *Creation of* Adam, *from Peter Comestor,* Historia scholastica *(orig. compiled twelfth century), Bohemia, early fifteenth century. Vatican City, Biblioteca Apostolica Vaticana, Vat. Lat. 5697, fol.13r.*

trees that were 'pleasant to the sight and good for food' (verse 9). In the middle of the garden were two special trees, the Tree of Life and the Tree of the Knowledge of Good and Evil, and four rivers sprang forth to water the garden. Then God noticed that of all the creatures he had created, man alone lacked a mate. He caused Adam to fall into a deep sleep, and then shaped a woman from one of his ribs (Fig 19). When Adam awoke, he found himself with a companion, Eve. Entrusting to Adam the care of a garden that provided the perfect conditions for human life (Fig 20), God ordered the pair never to touch the fruit growing on the Tree of the Knowledge of Good and Evil. Eve, however, yielded to the serpent's temptation, plucked a forbidden fruit, ate of it and gave some to her husband (Fig 21). For their disobedience, man and woman were expelled forever from the Garden of Eden (Fig 22).

This account has left biblical commentators with puzzling questions. Did Adam and Eve's garden really exist on earth? What exactly was it, and where was it? The interpretation was made more difficult by a complex textual transmission. An ancient oral tradition was probably written down in Hebrew in the ninth or tenth

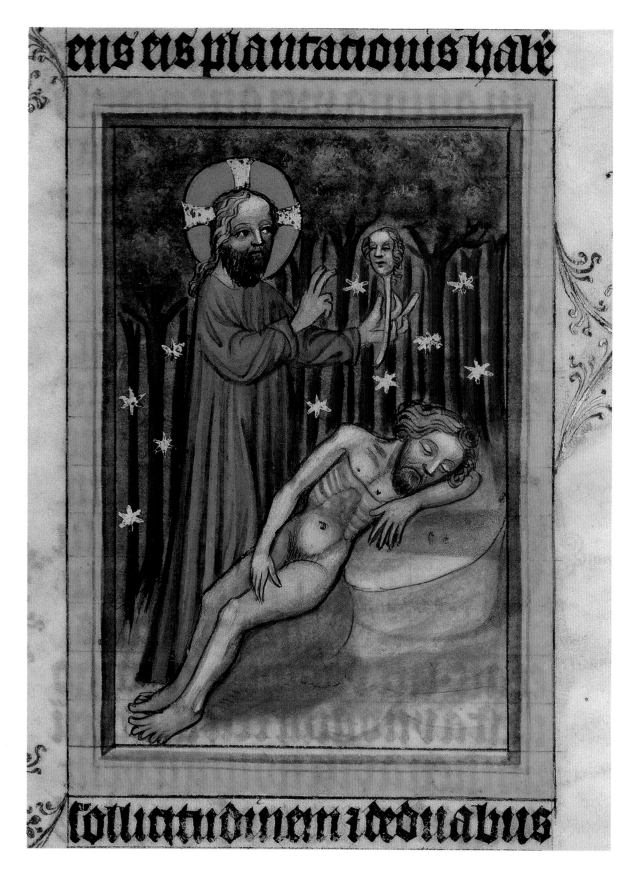

Fig 19 (opposite) Creation of Eve, *from Peter Comestor,* Historia scholastica *(orig. compiled twelfth century), Bohemia, early fifteenth century. Vatican City, Biblioteca Apostolica Vaticana, Vat. Lat. 5697, fol.16r.*

Fig 20 (above left) Adam and Eve in the Garden of Eden, *from Peter Comestor,* Historia scholastica *(orig. compiled twelfth century), Bohemia, early fifteenth century. Vatican City, Biblioteca Apostolica Vaticana, Vat. Lat. 5697, fol.17r.*

Fig 21 (above right) The Fall, *from Peter Comestor,* Historia scholastica *(orig. compiled twelfth century), Bohemia, early fifteenth century. Vatican City, Biblioteca Apostolica Vaticana, Vat. Lat. 5697, fol.17v.*

century BC, but this text has been lost and the authoritative Hebrew version is the work of medieval Jewish scholars. As we have seen, a Greek translation of the first five books of the lost original Hebrew text became available in the third century BC in Egypt for Greek-speaking Jews, the version today known as the Septuagint (p.10). A number of fragmentary Latin translations of biblical passages from the Septuagint circulated in the early centuries of Christianity, becoming known as the *Vetus Latina* (the Old Latin). Early in the fifth century AD St Jerome provided the standard and authoritative Latin version for Western Christians, now known as the Vulgate.

Problems of translation and interpretation in the absence of an original standard version have led to a tangle of assumptions. For example, *eden* in Hebrew means 'delight', as many biblical scholars liked to point out. However, the term could be taken either as a common noun to indicate the pleasure of the garden (as Jerome did) or as a proper noun to designate a specific place called Eden (as in the Septuagint). Moreover, the Hebrew qualifies *gan eden* with the term *miq-qedem* – a word that has two quite different meanings, one referring to space, the other to time. The translators of the Septuagint and the *Vetus Latina* chose to give the expression its spatial meaning, stating that God planted paradise in the east. In contrast, Jerome chose to render the Hebrew temporally, conveying the idea that the earthly paradise had been created at the beginning.

Another problem concerned the identity of the four rivers that watered the Garden of Eden. Two of them, the Tigris and the Euphrates, were easily recognised. The other two rivers, the Pison and the Gihon, posed greater problems of identification. The most common interpretation, originally put forward by the first-century Jewish historian Flavius Josephus (*Jewish Antiquities*, I.37–39), was to identify the Pison and the Gihon with the Ganges and the Nile respectively. But how could they all come from a single source?

From the early debate on the nature and location of the Garden of Eden described in Genesis came two main approaches, one allegorical and one literal. To explain the duplication of the story of man's creation (in the first chapter an ideal being made in the image of God, in the second a fallen creature banished from Eden), a Platonic interpretation of Genesis distinguished a heavenly, immortal and godlike human being (the true human nature) from its shadow – an earthly, sinful and corruptible man, confined within a physical body, who had the task to return to his original and spiritual perfection.

Scholars who read Genesis as Platonic philosophers attempted to reveal deeper meanings hidden in the text. In their view, the garden of Adam and Eve stood for the human soul, while the trees in the garden were the virtues planted in man by God. The four rivers were the four cardinal virtues (Prudence, Fortitude, Temperance and Justice). Eden, that is 'delight', symbolised the ecstasy that a soul finds in the service of the Lord. The events described in Genesis were taken as referring to processes within the soul, disclosing the pattern of all human sin: Adam, figuratively the human mind, had been instructed to pursue the virtues (represented by the Tree of Life and the other trees). Eve, born when Adam fell asleep (that is, when the mind was off-guard), symbolised the physical senses. She was corrupted by pleasure, represented by the serpent, and seduced Adam; and the Tree of Life became the Tree of Knowledge.

Other Christian exegetes (the interpreters of the sacred text), however, saw things differently. They believed that those who brought philosophical principles to bear on the biblical narrative contradicted the Word of God. To doubt the historicity of the events narrated in the Bible implied that Scripture could be questioned by human reason; and to deny the historical existence of Adam and Eve and the story of their Fall was to put the whole system of Christian dogma at risk. God had created paradise somewhere in the east, in the place described in the Bible, and, in honour of man, he had planted therein real trees therein. Real waters flowed out of it, travelling underground and turning into the four great rivers of the world. Adam and Eve were real people, from whom all subsequent generations were descended. Whereas the allegorical reading elevated Eden from the realm of geography into a spiritual dimension, the literal interpretation produced a story and a geography of paradise tied closely to the plane of human history and to the physical earth.

In the fifth century St Augustine provided an authoritative solution to this opposition, working out an exegetical, or explanatory, framework that put the notion of an earthly paradise beyond controversy. Against the threats from various heresies, Augustine was keen to demonstrate the goodness of the visible creation, and to reject any dualistic opposition between soul and body and between an original – heavenly and godlike – perfection and the lower world of materiality. In his view God did not create two beings, a heavenly as opposed to an earthly Adam, but just one man, perfect in mind and body. He suggested that a single, instantaneous creation out of time (described in the first chapter of Genesis as a week to adapt the mystery to the capacity of the human mind) was followed by a creation within time (described in the second chapter). Therefore the man formed from the dust of the ground, and referred to in the second chapter, was God's fulfilment in time of the being in his own image that he had been envisaging in the extra-temporal creation related in the first chapter.

This theological view implied important aspects. Human nature was not intrinsically imperfect, but created perfect by God. The visible world was no mere reflection of a higher reality, but the work of an omnipotent creator and the stage on which God's plan for the salvation of humankind was to be enacted. Adam was a corporeal creature, a real man in the flesh, placed in a real and corporeal paradise. Moreover, for Augustine, Scripture had divine authority. God spoke to mankind through the events recorded in the Bible. Its words were to be taken literally, but they were also figurative signs, alluding to things that in turn signified something else. As with anything in the Old Testament, for Christians the real Garden of Eden and the true story of the Fall referred, as signs, to Christian realities. Adam prefigured Christ, Eve foreshadowed the Virgin Mary and the Fall was part of God's salvation plan. Eden anticipated the Church, the Christian soul and the final paradise in heaven.

Augustine's rejection of dualism and deep sense of history, his insistence on the transcendent importance of Scripture and his combination of the literal and the allegorical approaches created the conditions for understanding the Garden of Eden as a specific place on earth (Fig 23). Augustine was not himself particularly interested in geographical matters, but his theological concerns and his emphasis on history produced the geographical assumptions about the location of Eden that preoccupied theologians and mapmakers for centuries afterwards.

NAMING THE PLACE

The grounds for identifying the site of the earthly paradise rested on the *Vetus Latina* (the old Latin translation of the Hebrew text of Genesis) which, as we have seen, had explained that paradise had been planted 'in the east'. The question of the whereabouts of the Garden, of secondary importance for Augustine, caught the imagination of later biblical exegetes who drew out of Augustine's writings the latent geographical discourse and who named the place where mapmakers could put paradise.

In the seventh century Isidore, bishop of Seville, included the earthly paradise, surrounded by a wall of fire, among the regions of Asia. A century later Bede, the scholar monk of Jarrow and Monkwearmouth, both in the kingdom of Northumbria, wrote that the eastern Eden was kept separate from the rest of the world by a vast expanse of land or sea, and was at such an altitude that it had survived untouched by the Flood that covered the rest of the earth. Notwithstanding the divine veiling of the precise location of paradise, Bede went so far as to suggest that the land of Havilah – described in the Bible as bordering paradise and surrounded by the River Pison (Genesis 2.11) – was a region in India. Bede saw a clear match between Scripture, which portrayed Havilah as a land rich in gold, and Pliny the Elder's *Naturalis historia*, which stated the same about India (VI.21–24). Both Isidore and Bede were in accord

with the traditional idea, taken up earlier by Augustine, that the four rivers flowed underground from paradise to the inhabited world.

As shown by two highly influential twelfth-century texts, the anonymous *Glossa ordinaria* and Peter Lombard's *Sententiae*, medieval theology had by then settled on the essentials of Eden: paradise was a real place on earth, inaccessible because of original sin, yet connected to the inhabited world through the four rivers. The Garden of Eden was out of sight, but very probably situated somewhere in the remotest eastern corner of Asia, at an exceedingly high altitude and thus untouched by the Flood.

The corollary of the geographical location of the earthly paradise, however, is its place in human history, and its inextricable association with the entire scheme of Christian salvation. Although Eden was inaccessible and forbidden to mankind, the Garden remained paradoxically present by its loss. The historical process set in motion by God was designed to repair the damages of original sin, and the lost paradise was seen as a prefiguration of both the Christian community on earth and the final paradise in heaven.

MAPPING WITH THEOLOGY

The challenge for the Christian compilers of maps was to combine geographical knowledge with the biblical world view. Belief in an earthly Eden urged them to render visible in their world maps a place that was geographically inaccessible (yet linked to the inhabited earth by the four rivers) and remote in time (yet still relevant as the scene of an essential episode of salvation history). A process of Christianisation of classical geography had been taking place since the early centuries of the Christian era. Traditional geographical ideas about the dimensions of the globe, its division into parts and the listing of the peoples and provinces of the inhabited world were adopted and refined to accommodate Christian themes, a process in which the Garden of Eden featured prominently.

For the scribes and artists responsible for the maps, the history of salvation brought about a corresponding geography of salvation. Most of the biblical places – specific points on earth where, according to the Bible, God's intervention had taken place - were locatable in well known regions. Although very different from our modern representations of the earth, however, medieval maps were not devotional, pastoral or theological documents. Nor were they tools of religious propaganda or sermons in visual form. Rather, they were representations of the world according to a particular conception, one that took into account the scriptural text and the teachings of the Christian faith. Assessed on their own terms, the medieval maps of the world were in fact no less scientific than any other type of map.

Today, more than two centuries after the Enlightenment, it is sometimes difficult to understand how the Bible was read in earlier times, and to grasp the degree to which mapmaking was related to theology and biblical exegesis. Since the rise of modern science, the tendency has been to see the Bible as a specifically religious book; but for Christian scholars of the past the Bible provided not only religious guidance, but

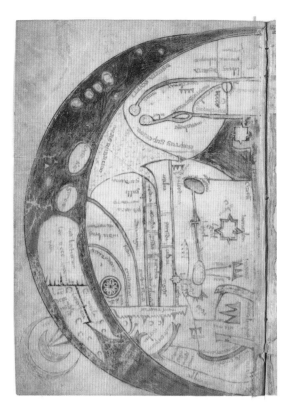
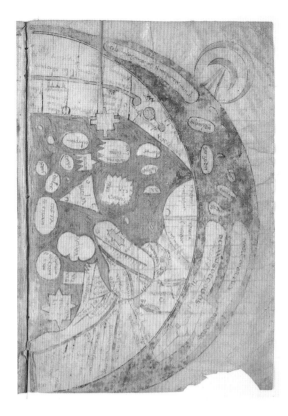

Fig 24 *The Vatican (or Pseudo–Isidorean) map, Italy or southern France, late eighth century. Vatican City, Biblioteca Apostolica Vaticana, MS Vat. Lat. 6018, fols.63v–64r.*

also the key to *all* forms of knowledge. The Bible was the authoritative account of the world's creation and the history of the human race. Specific geographical learning could be taken from other texts, but it had to be adapted to fit a biblical world view.

The 'Pseudo–Isidorean Vatican map' (so-called from its current location in the Biblioteca Apostolica Vaticana and from its former attribution, now disproved, to Isidore of Seville) bears witness to the process by which Christians filtered classical learning to fit their beliefs (Fig 24). Drawn, probably, in Italy or southern France, and probably in the late eighth century, the map has a distinctly classical imprint that has been modified by the inclusion of biblical material. The left half of the map shows Asia, Egypt and the lands of Canaan and the other lands of biblical history; the Garden of Eden is clearly seen in the east, marked by a circle containing a floret. The right half of the map shows the heartlands of the Graeco-Roman civilisation.

The point of the mapmaker was that humankind's history and geography had been unified by the universal message of Christianity. Chronological and computational material follows the world map in the codex to show how time was regulated by the movement of the sun and the moon in relation to the earth. An explicit link between the map and the subsequent astronomical tables is suggested by the astral signs depicted in the map's northeastern and southwestern corners. In contemporary terms, the Vatican map was no less 'scientific' in its preoccupation with the location of paradise, and in its wealth of allusions to the Bible, than in its highlighting of the role of sun and moon as tidal forces, or in its depiction of other aspects of the world's geography.

Visual Interlude
Paradise on the Beatus Map

◆

At more or less the same time as the anonymous scribe in Italy or France was sketching the Vatican map, a Benedictine monk in northern Spain was creating another a map of the world. He was Beatus of Liébana, in Asturia, and the work was designed to illustrate his commentary on the Book of Revelation. No less than the Vatican map, Beatus's map, on which paradise is featured much more prominently, was also a summary of the Christian vision of history. It underlined the theme of Beatus's *Commentary on the Apocalypse of Saint John*, in which he urged fellow-Christians to keep their minds fixed on the heavenly kingdom. Beatus, like other Christian exegetes, held that God's final victory over evil, prophesied in the Book of Revelation, had already taken place through Christ's incarnation,

sacrifice on the Cross and resurrection, and with the establishment of the Christian Church at Pentecost. Christ's second coming and the final and full establishment of heaven on earth was still to come, but the Heavenly City, prepared as a bride for her husband (Revelation 21.2), came down to earth each day through faith and the observance of a Christian life.

Beatus's cartographical portrait of the earth was an integral part of his theological argument. In the section dealing with the universality of the Christian Church, Beatus invited his reader to contemplate the map and see how the apostles evangelised the earth, performing signs and miracles throughout the world. The apostles were the 12 gates and the 12 foundations of the Heavenly Jerusalem (Revelation

Fig 25 (left) *Map of the world, from a manuscript of Beatus of Liébana's* In Apocalypsin, *Shahagún, Navarra, 1086. Burgo de Osma, Archivo de la Catedral, MS 1, fols.34v–35r.*

Fig 26 (opposite) *Map of the world, from a manuscript of Beatus of Liébana's* In Apocalypsin, *Catalonia, probably Ripoll, early twelfth century. Turin, Biblioteca Nazionale Universitaria, MS I.II.1, fols.45v–46r.*

21.12): the map portrayed the apocalyptic period (after the Incarnation of Christ) in which all the regions and lands of the earth became the holy field of divine action.

The map that accompanied Beatus's original manuscript has not survived. Instead, we know of 14 copies in manuscripts dating from the tenth to the thirteenth centuries. On the map in a manuscript of 1086, now in the library of the cathedral in Burgo de Osma, Spain, and characterised by its oval shape and portraits of the apostles in their respective fields of mission, Eden is indicated by a geometric design with the four rivers, reinforcing the idea of the diffusion of Christianity over the earth (Fig 25). Beatus himself compared the four rivers issuing from a single source to the four Gospels issuing from the single mouth of Christ; both rivers and Gospels bring life to the world.

On other Beatus manuscripts, Eden is marked by a narrative vignette that includes the figures of Adam and Eve. The circular, early twelfth-century map, from a manuscript copied in Catalonia, depicts all the main features of the paradise narrative – Adam and Eve, the Tree of Knowledge and the snake – without any enclosing rectangle or circle (Fig 26). Interestingly, on this map the River Jordan, in which Christ was baptised, and the mountains of Lebanon, which Beatus called a symbol of baptismal purity, are shown in the immediate vicinity of the site of the Fall, as a token of the purification of corrupted man by the new paradise of the Church. Another twelfth-century version of the map, in a manuscript

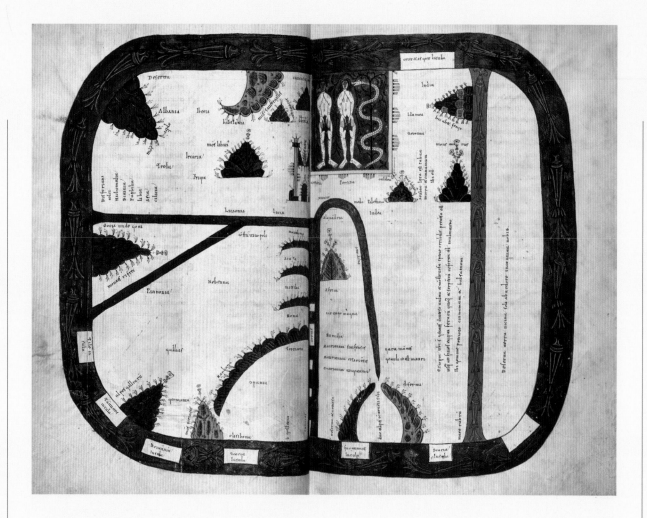

copied in the library of the Abbey of Santo Domingo de Silos, in northern Spain, rectangular in outline, presents Adam and Eve in a rectangular paradise (Fig 27). Its portrayal of Adam and Eve is also significant in making the link between the origin of the world's population in Adam and its conversion to Christianity through the work of the apostles. The ocean that surrounds the earth is shown as full of fish, a possible allusion to the apostolic task of fishing for men (Matthew 4.19; Mark 1.17; Luke 5.10), intended to emphasise the dissemination of Christianity.

As the reader may already have surmised, the incorporation of paradise on medieval world maps, far from being a naive depiction of some picturesque fantasy land, epitomised a vital

Fig 27 *Map of the world, from a manuscript of Beatus of Liébana's* In Apocalypsin, *Monastery of Santo Domingo de Silos, 1106. London, British Library, Add. MS 11695, fols 39v–40r.*

element of Christian doctrine. The Garden of Eden signified far more than a mythical state of innocence or a fanciful dreamland, forever lost. The earthly paradise pointed to a present and future reality, that of Christian redemption.

Bibliographic Essay

◆

Several biblical encyclopedias clarify the problems of Genesis's textual transmission, including Wilfrid R. F. Browning, *A Dictionary of the Bible* (Oxford: Oxford University Press, 1996); Cecil Roth, ed., *Encyclopaedia Judaica*, 17 vols (Jerusalem: Encyclopaedia Judaica, 1972); Johannes B. Bauer, ed., *Encyclopedia of Biblical Theology*, 3 vols (London–Sydney: Sheed and Ward, 1970); Matthew Black and Harold H. Rowley, eds., *Peake's Commentary on the Bible* (London: Nelson, 1962); and Bruce M. Metzen and Michael D. Coogan, eds., *The Oxford Companion to the Bible* (New York–Oxford: Oxford University Press, 1993).

For the debate about the Garden of Eden, useful and well informed surveys are provided by Monique Alexandre, 'Entre ciel et terre: les premiers débats sur le site du Paradis (Gen. 2, 8–15 et ses réceptions)', in François Jouan and Bernard Deforge, eds., *Peuples et pays mythiques* (Paris: Belles Lettres, 1988), pp.187–224; and, for the medieval period up to 1200, Reinhold R. Grimm, *Paradisus coelestis, paradisus terrestris: zur Auslegungsgeschichte des Paradieses im Abendland bis um 1200* (Munich: Fink, 1977). Augustine developed his arguments on the Garden of Eden mostly in his *De Genesi ad litteram* and *De civitate Dei*; Isidore and Bede in their *Etymologiae* and *Libri quatuor in principium Genesis usque ad nativitatem Isaac et electionem Ismahelis adnotationum* respectively.

By way of an introduction to the extensive literature on Christian biblical exegesis see Beryl Smalley, *The Study of the Bible in the Middle Ages*, 3rd edn (Oxford: Basil Blackwell, 1984); Henri de Lubac, *Exégèse médiévale: Les quatre sens de l'Écriture*, 4 vols (Paris: Aubier, 1959–64); Jean Daniélou, *Sacramentum futuri: études sur les origines de la typologie biblique* (Paris: Beauchesne, 1950), Wulstan Hibberd, trans.: *From Shadows to Reality.*

Studies in the Biblical Typology of the Fathers (London: Burns & Oates, 1960). For a thorough overview on the Christianisation of classical geographical knowledge see Hervé Inglebert, *Interpretatio Christiana. Les mutations des savoirs (cosmographie, géographie, ethnographie, histoire) dans l'Antiquité chrétienne: 30–630 après J.-C.* (Paris: Institut d'Études Augustiniennes, 2001).

Transcriptions of the legends on the Pseudo-Isidorean Vatican Map are found in François Glorie, ed., 'Mappa mundi e codice Vatic. Lat. 6018', in *Itineraria et alia geographica*, *Corpus Christianorum, Series Latina* CLXXV (Turnhout: Brepols, 1965), pp.455–66; and Richard Uhden, 'Die Weltkarte des Isidorus von Sevilla', *Mnemosyne: Bibliotheca Classica Batavia*, 3rd series, III (1935–36), pp.1–28. See also Leonid S. Chekin, 'Easter Tables and the Pseudo-Isidorean Vatican Map', *Imago Mundi*, 51 (1999), pp.13–23; Evelyn Edson, *Mapping Time and Space: How Medieval Mapmakers Viewed Their World* (London: The British Library, 1997; 1999), pp.61–4; Edson, 'World Maps and Easter Tables: Medieval Maps in Context', *Imago Mundi*, 48 (1996), pp.30–2; Patrick Gautier Dalché, 'De la glose à la contemplation. Place et fonction de la carte dans les manuscrits du haut Moyen Âge' in *Testo e immagine nell'Alto Medioevo*, 2 vols (Spoleto: Centro italiano di studi sull'Alto Medioevo, 1994), II, pp.759–61.

For Beatus of Liébana, see Eugenio Romero, ed., *Commentarius in Apocalypsin*, Pose, 2 vols (Rome: Istituto Poligrafico e Zecca dello Stato, 1985); and John Williams, *The Illustrated Beatus: A Corpus of the Illustrations in the Commentary on the Apocalypse*, 5 vols (London: Harvey Miller, 1994–2003) and Williams, 'Isidore, Orosius and the Beatus Map', *Imago Mundi*, 49 (1997), pp.7–32.

CHAPTER 4

MAPPING TIME

Three monks are walking by a river, following its course to wherever it might lead, attracted by the multi-coloured branch of a wonderful tree they had seen floating on it. Unbeknown to them, the stream is one of the four rivers of the earthly paradise. All of a sudden, they find themselves in a wondrous garden, into which a blazing figure – an angel – beckons them. When, overwhelmed by their surroundings and by the magnificence they see all around them, the monks humbly ask for permission to remain in the garden for a fortnight, a peal of laughter resounds through the grove, and they realise that they have been there for hundreds of years already.

FROM A FOURTEENTH-CENTURY
ITALIAN LEGEND

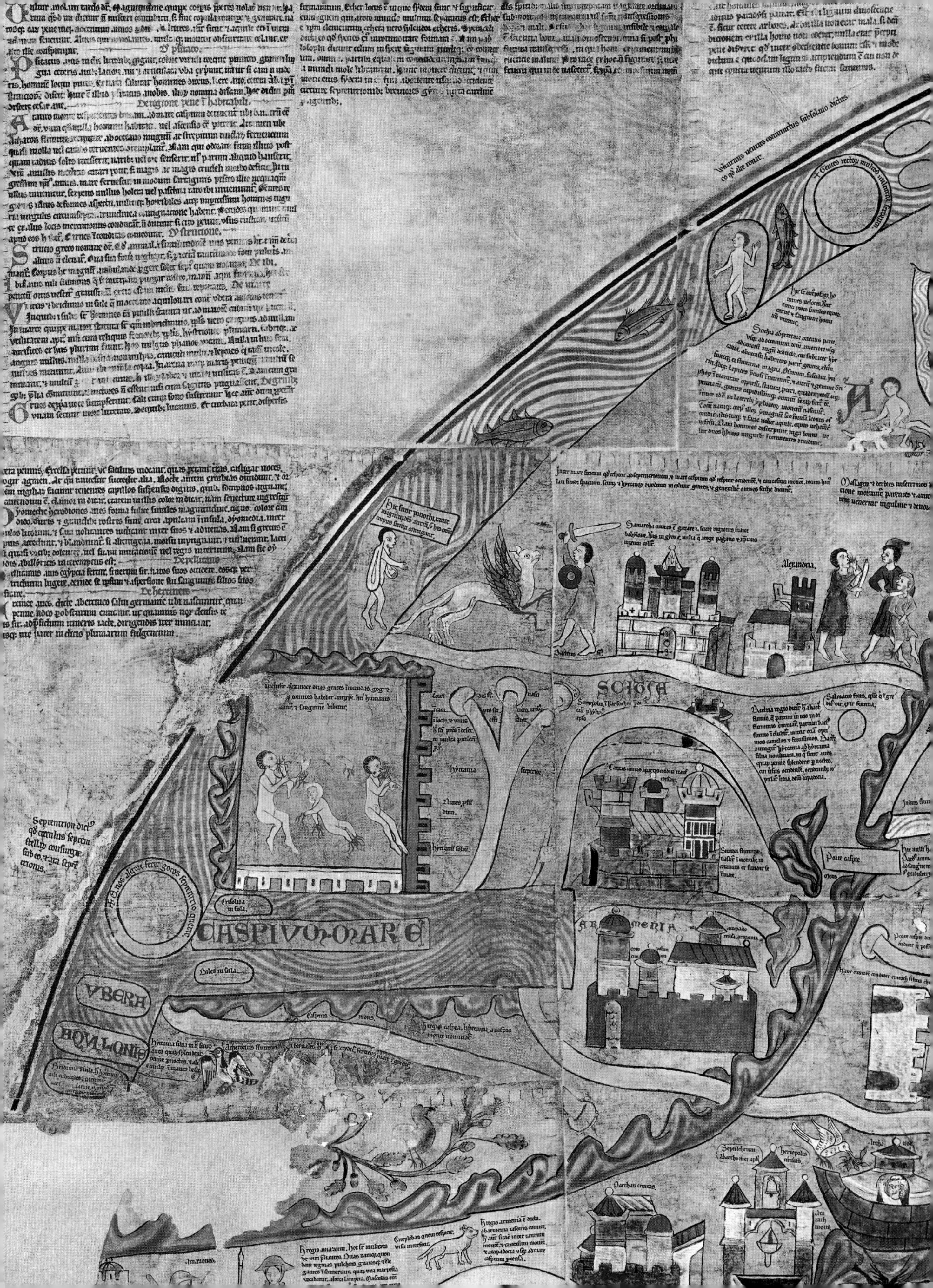

CASPIVM MARE

SCITIA

ARMENIA

ABERII

AQVILONIS

Alexandria

MAPS OF THE WORLD: MEDIEVAL AND MODERN

Fig 28 *The Sawley world map, Durham, England, late twelfth century. Cambridge, Parker Library, Corpus Christi College, MS 66, p.2.*

Google Earth allows you to fly to any part of the globe. At a click of the mouse, you can zoom from your own home into the most impenetrable of mountain chains or to the remotest of islands. In your mind, you can stroll along the streets of the foreign cities of the world before returning home to see your own garden on the screen. You can switch from panoramic satellite imagery to the intimacy of the ground level view maps, and from abstraction to reality: satellite technology and radar electronics have combined to give you maps of the earth seen from beyond the earth. However, each map is a view of the earth at a specific moment. Like every modern map of the world, even *Google Maps* captures the world only at a particular point in time.

The medieval view of the world was quite different. The world maps (or *mappae mundi* in Latin) common in Western Europe between the twelfth and fourteenth centuries had a wider scope (Fig 28). These maps show not only the world's geography, but also the whole of human history from the Christian standpoint. A medieval *mappa mundi* is far more than a spatial facsimile of the earth such as *Google Earth*. It projects historical events on to a geographical framework, and it makes it possible for the human eye to embrace, as from a higher viewpoint, the space–time continuum of history, from beginning to end. The aim of the medieval compilers of these maps was nothing less than to portray an orderly physical and human geography, and to make visible and comprehensible the invisible order that guides the course of human events.

Modern readers, however, are more familiar with a map that does not aim to show historical time, but that plots the earth on to a framework of parallels and meridians, measured lines constructed from astronomical data. This type of world map, described in the second century AD by the Alexandrian geographer Claudius Ptolemaeus (Ptolemy), provided the basis of Renaissance as well as modern cartography. On the Ptolemaic map, space is structured and defined by mathematical measurement; places are located according to coordinates of latitude and longitude; and the spherical earth is portrayed on a flat surface by means of a geometrical projection. The objective is to include only contemporary features (Fig 62, p.102).

On a *mappa mundi*, in contrast, many layers of time are piled up on geographical space. The lasting influence on medieval scholars of Graeco-Roman geographies and histories ensured that the names of places whose day was long past remained common currency. Towns such as ancient Troy in Asia Minor and Leptis Magna and Carthage in North Africa remind us that mapped space can contain different chronologies, blending the historical with the contemporary. The names of classical peoples, ancient tribes, regions and cities jostle on the map with the names of new cities and nations. Next to the boundary lines of Roman provinces that delineate a vanished empire, such as Gallia, Germania, Achaea and Macedonia, are the names of thriving contemporary centres of learning and trade: Genoa, Venice, Bologna and Barcelona. The great cities of Rome and Constantinople betoken a glorious past, while places in the Middle East – evoking the life of Christ and his apostles

(Jerusalem, Bethlehem, Nazareth, the Sea of Galilee, Damascus, Ephesus, Antioch, Tarsus) – point to a different glory. From still earlier in biblical history come the names of the Twelve Tribes of Israel, the Tower of Babel, Babylon, Mount Sinai, the Red Sea, the sons of Noah, the Ark and paradise. Between 1100 and 1400 mapmakers sought to feature the Christian perspective of all human time and all earthly space on their *mappae mundi*. They were not the first to appreciate the intermingling of history and geography, however. Even earlier Jewish, Greek and Roman writers had already been aware of the interrelationship of time and space.

Thus medieval European mapmakers incorporated the history of human development into their world picture, using geographical space to indicate events from different times. They did not deploy a universal system of map signs arranged in mathematical order, but depicted neighbouring places and events next to each other, without concern for the exact distance or direction between them. To them the crucial factor in the structure and content of *mappae mundi* was history, not geography. Whereas they knew a great deal about world history, they knew less about the details of world geography, about which there were many uncertainties. What, for example, enclosed the *oecumene*, the part of the earth that they inhabited? In contrast history had a precise beginning (in Eden). It had passed through a sequence of numbered ages (one to five, marked by crucial tests such as the Flood and Abraham's sacrifice) and was heading (in the present sixth age, beginning with the Incarnation of Christ) for a pre-determined end. Just as the world had been created in six days, with God resting on the seventh, so the six ages of human history would be followed by eternal rest in heaven. Geography was the servant to history, and world maps were world chronicles.

On a medieval *mappa mundi*, a place took its importance from the event that had occurred there. Human settlements and natural features – rivers, mountains, seas, islands, lakes and forests – provided important markers of the historical event. Just as the *mappa mundi* shows not simply a place but an 'event-place', so it also portrays 'epochal zones': strata defined by a set of contemporary event-places (for example, the ancient Persian and Macedonian empires). East is placed at the top, in the direction of the rising sun, in contrast to the Ptolemaic map which, as a consequence of its astronomically defined structure, usually has north at the top (Fig 62).

Whereas the coordinates of a Ptolemaic map ensure the mathematically correct positioning of every point on the map, each place having an equal value, different cartographical rules applied to the *mappa mundi*. It was no less important to the medieval mapmaker to mark a place accurately, but its positioning on the map was governed by the rule of contiguity, not mathematically measured distance or direction. Likewise whereas map signs on a modern map are graded mathematically, on a medieval *mappa mundi* the manner of presenting each event-place depended on its cultural or historical importance: a large labyrinth, for example, indicated the island of Crete or the portrayal of St Anthony marked the Egyptian desert. The significance of a place in world history could be emphasised by exaggerating the size of the sign, as in the case of the Tower of Babel or the cities of Jerusalem and Rome.

What mattered to the compiler of a *mappa mundi* was the intrinsic importance of each event-place. Historically important event-places were positioned on the map irrespective of the size of the features themselves or the distance on the ground between them. Since the map was not to be used for finding the way (medieval travellers used itineraries rather than maps), the lack of mathematical accuracy did not matter. A map featuring paradise was not expected to indicate any physical way of reaching it, but only to point to a location that was the scene of a critical episode in salvation history and an integral element of the cosmos (Fig 29).

Fig 29 *The smaller map of the world, from Ranulf Higden's* Polychronicon, *Ramsey, England, c.1350. London, British Library, Royal MS 14.C.IX, fol.2v. (See Fig 104 at the end of the book for the larger and more detailed map.)*

PARADISE ON THE MAP

The inclusion of paradise on a *mappa mundi* was not, as was sometimes thought, the expression of a bizarre superstition that vanished at the dawn of the modern era. According to that post-Enlightenment view, a *mappa mundi* was a crude sketch made by a fearful monk to impress the common people with irrational fables of monsters and marvels, or to promote a religious fantasy. Modern thinking, however, no longer sees the *mappa mundi* as the product of the naive cartography of a medieval 'dark age', just as it no longer has uncritical faith in the notion of scientific and objective geography. Nor was the depiction of paradise an evocation of some fantasy land, but rather a way of accommodating an event-place essential in human history, setting the original sin of Adam and Eve in the place where it occurred. It was hard, a couple of centuries ago, to appreciate that the mathematically scaled map is not the only valid kind of map. We now recognise that maps are inevitably a reflection of the culture in which they are produced, and that mapping may involve time as well as space; it may also represent ideas about the wider cosmos that cannot be experienced directly.

The cartography that had no difficulty in including paradise on a map was obviously a cartography different from our own. In fact, *only* a map that allows for the temporal as well the spatial dimension – and a map that ignores the mathematical measurement of distance – can locate the unlocatable and feature the inaccessible in this way. For the medieval compilers of *mappae mundi*, paradise was a highly relevant cartographical feature. They recognised that paradise was inaccessible from the inhabited earth, despite its contiguity, but they conceived it as part of a well-defined temporal structure in which places were linked to each other by historical rather than spatial relationships. Paradise on a map was not intended to convey a location defined by latitude and longitude. It sought rather to remind the observer of its proximity to the inhabited earth and its relevance to human history (Fig 30).

MAPPING TIME AND SPACE

Much of our vocabulary for time is spatial, while that for space is temporal. We talk about a 'distant' event, for example, and a 'succession' of objects. In the Middle Ages, however, the correspondence between time and space was far more than a metaphor, and the compilers of *mappae mundi* were demonstrating their intuition for the 'space-time' character of reality. The medieval conception of the interplay between space and time was different from that of the post-Renaissance period, when space and time were seen as absolute and universal properties, independent from each other. In the Middle Ages, by contrast, map makers acknowledged that geographical space cannot exist without time. Their sophisticated recognition of this interdependency seems to be consistent with discoveries in modern physics, in particular with Einstein's theories of relativity, the view that all space and time measurements are relative and depend on the observer, and that gravity makes space–time curved.

Fig 30 *The Evesham world map, Evesham Abbey, Gloucestershire, c.1390–1415. London, College of Arms, Muniment Room 18/19.*

59

The nature of space and time, and the mystery of their relationship, have been investigated at least since the time of ancient Greek philosophy. In the twentieth century, however, Einstein has made clear with a mathematical model that space and time are inseparable, and are intimately connected in a four-dimensional reality. It may be argued that a similar point had already been made in the twelfth century by the theologian and exegete Hugh of Saint Victor, who taught that God's plan for humankind had unfolded, and was still unfolding, through time and space. According to Hugh, a spatially ordered sequence of historical events followed a preordained transfer of human imperial power and cultural excellence. The sequence ran from east to west. History had begun in the extreme east of the world, where God had put Adam into an earthly paradise, and the historical centre of gravity (comprising the most important events, as defined according to a global perspective) moved progressively westwards, following the sun's daily course. History was proceeding from the Orient to the Occident, from Adam to Christ, from the early kingdoms in the eastern regions to the Roman empire, and so towards its culmination in the passion of Christ in Jerusalem.

Jerusalem – the navel of the world, at the centre of both history and geography – marked the beginning of the end: the opening of the final phase, the time of waiting for the final revelation of the kingdom of God. This final time would coincide with the margins of space, namely the most extreme confines of Western Europe and the Mediterranean basin, as geographical extension and historical progression went together. Now, in Hugh's day, the sequence of the major events of human history had reached the extremity of the world as space (that is, in the West), at the moment in which humankind was about to reach the end of the world as time.

The idea of the progression of history from east to west lies at the heart of the medieval *mappa mundi*. Hugh's vision provides us with a unique key for understanding the medieval *mappa mundi* as a map of historical process rather than a static picture of the earth, with the portrayal of paradise on the eastern edge of Asia marking the beginning of time. The *mappae mundi* of his time, and after, presented an overview of human history open to the future, the end of that history.

A CASE IN POINT: THE HEREFORD MAPPA MUNDI

The fundamental east–west progression that structured the *mappae mundi* gave them a more or less standard internal structure and a common basic content. An outstanding example of the mosaic of event-places and epochal zones ordered historically from east to west is provided by a map, made about 1300, now in Hereford Cathedral (Figs 31 and 32). This world map has the 'T–O' structure typical of many maps of the period. The sphere of the inhabited Old World, surrounded by the outer ocean (the 'O'), is divided into three parts by lines representing the River Tanais (the Don, the traditional boundary between Europe and Asia), the River Nile (the boundary between Africa and Asia) and the Mediterranean Sea (the boundary between Europe

Fig 31 (opposite and overleaf)
The Hereford world map,
Lincoln (?and Hereford),
c.1300. Hereford Cathedral.

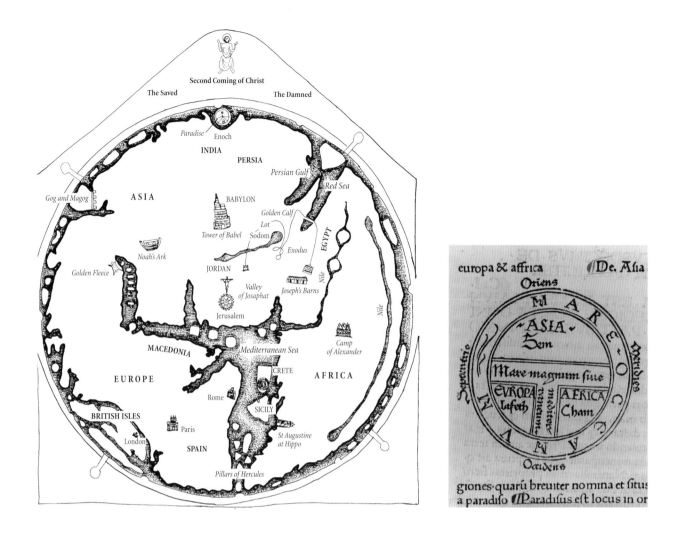

Fig 32 (above left) *Diagram of the Hereford world map.*

Fig 33 (above) *'T–O' map, from Isidore of Seville,* Etymologiae *(orig. compiled c.620), (Augsburg: Guntherus Ziner, 1472), unfoliated, but at 176v. London, British Library, IB.5441.*

and Africa) which formed the 'T' (Fig 33). In the extreme east, at the top of the map, is the island of paradise, on which is a walled garden where Adam and Eve are eating the forbidden fruit. The Tree of the Knowledge of Good and Evil shades the spring from which emerge the four rivers (Fig 34).

The Hereford map may seem picturesque with its monsters, cannibals, sirens and fabulous animals; certainly a vast and weird array of natural wonders, drawn from late classical sources, especially Pliny, is depicted (Figs 35 and 36). The Red Sea is duly painted red, but the outlines of countries, seas and rivers are not all easy to recognise. The author of the map, however, knew perfectly what he was doing. Not by accident did Richard of Haldingham, acknowledged on the map as the author, refer to his work as a 'history'. He made sure that his map shows us clearly the progression of history from paradise, which marks the beginning in the east, to the Mediterranean Sea, which forms the central axis of the lower, western part of the map.

Below the earthly paradise is seen the first city, Enoch, founded by Cain before the Flood. Farther down is Noah's Ark, stranded on the mountains of Armenia (Fig 37). Then comes the Tower of Babel in Mesopotamia (Fig 38), with Abraham's city of Ur, in Chaldaea, nearby. Farther along are Joseph's barns in Egypt (Fig 39), the sinuous line of the Israelites' Exodus from Egypt to the Promised Land (Fig 40), Mount

Sinai, Jerusalem and a number of features associated with the New Testament. In the middle of the map, in Jerusalem, at the centre of both space and time, Christ is crucified (Fig 41). The east–west ordering of human history is further emphasised by rulers, peoples and monuments of the ancient empires. Significantly, no attempt was made to represent Asia in contemporary terms. There was no need to do so, for each region had had its own moment of importance on the continuum of world history and its own place on the world stage; and by the end of the thirteenth century the weight of history had already long shifted west to Europe.

The line of progression from east to west linked the remote beginning of time, in a distant eastern paradise, by way of an Asia of the past to the present in Europe and around the Mediterranean world. Here the east–west axis of human history has been expanded to encompass the parts of the northern hemisphere closest in time and space to the compiler of the map, Europe and North Africa. In this western area was the

Fig 34 (right) *Detail of Fig 31: the earthly paradise.*

Fig 35 (below right) *Detail of Fig 31: a monster.*

Fig 36 (below far right) *Detail of Fig 31: a siren.*

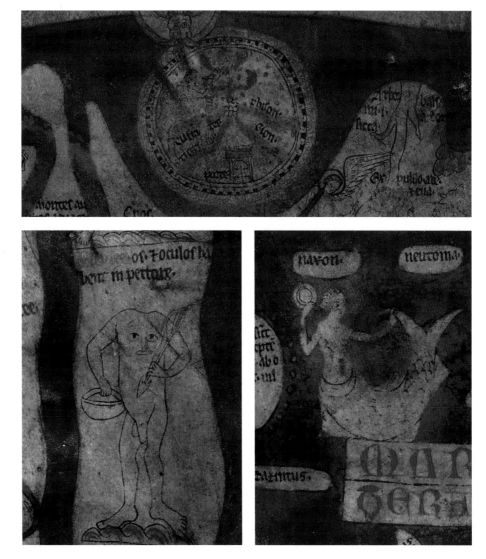

final epochal zone of the world, corresponding to the age inaugurated by the sacrifice of Christ in Jerusalem. During this age, starting from the central event–place on the map, the apostles had been dispatched to all three parts of the world to convert its peoples. At the bottom of the map are depicted the columns that, according to Greek mythology, were set up by Hercules at the westernmost limit of the Mediterranean to designate the end of the inhabited world. On the map, the Pillars of Hercules not only mark the final, western edge of the world in space, but also announce the end of the world in time (Fig 42).

In Asia, a note placed on a northern peninsula, enclosed by mountains and to the south by a wall, describes how the tribes of Gog and Magog were imprisoned behind the mountains by an earthquake and locked in by Alexander the Great's indestructible wall. The note warns of the horrifying customs of these fearsome peoples, who fed on human flesh and blood and who were destined to break out of their enclosure at the time of the Antichrist in order to devastate the world. As prophesied in the book of Revelation (20.7–8), the tribes of Gog and Magog will storm the world before the Day of Judgement. Their appearance on the map, as part of the inhabited world, yet separated from it by their temporary enclosure, is a concrete reference to the impending replacement of time by eternity. For the thirteenth-century observer of the Hereford *mappa mundi*, human history had reached its culmination. According to the map, the western progression of time had ceased and world space was filled to its limits. Signifying the imminence of God's fulfilment, the second coming of Christ in glory is shown at the apex of the map (Fig 43). The figure of Christ, shown in majesty judging the world and flanked by the saved and the damned, dominates the entire composition.

Fig 37 (top left) *Detail of Fig 31: Noah's Ark.*

Fig 38 (above) *Detail of Fig 31: the Tower of Babel.*

Fig 39 (above left) *Detail of Fig 31: Joseph's barns.*

Fig 40 (opposite, top left) *Detail of Fig 31: the Exodus.*

Fig 41 (opposite, top right) *Detail of Fig 31: Christ's Crucifixion in Jerusalem.*

Fig 42 (opposite, bottom left) *Detail of Fig 31: the Pillars of Hercules.*

Fig 43 (opposite, bottom right) *Detail of Fig 31: Christ in majesty.*

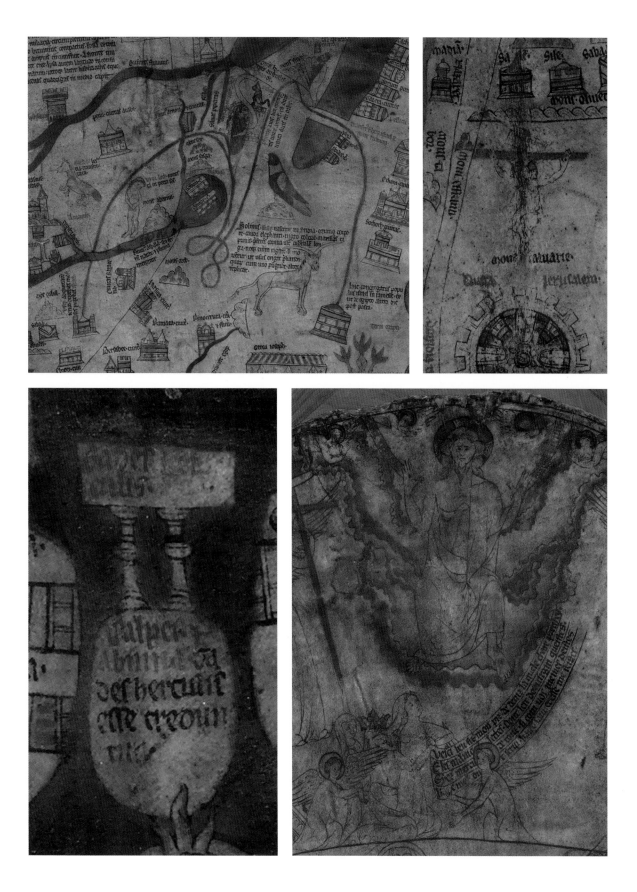

WHERE WAS EDEN?

The Hereford *mappa mundi* thus displayed the whole of human history, from the earthly paradise to the death and resurrection of Christ in Jerusalem and to his anticipated final triumph at the end of time. But where was paradise thought to be? As we have seen, in the Hebrew version of Genesis we read that God placed *gan Eden*, the Garden of Eden, *miq-qedem*. *Miq-qedem* indicates both when and where God had placed the Garden: it was 'at the beginning' (at the dawn of time) and 'in the east' (at the sunrise of space). Medieval cartographers too portrayed the paradise on the edge of the map, at the very boundary of time and space. There could be nothing on earth beyond a place that was both in the remotest past and the extreme east.

Paradise belonged to history, but it continued to exist, albeit inaccessible from the inhabited earth. Where exactly it was, nobody could ever know; and no living person would ever be allowed to reach it. After the Fall, the garden was guarded by the Cherubim's flaming sword, and separated from the inhabited earth by an impassable ocean and/or by a wall of fire, or by its site on the peak of an inaccessible mountain. As the Northumbrian monk Bede put it, 'there is no doubt that the place *was* and *is* on earth'. It was a place out of reach, but not entirely disconnected from the inhabited earth, as from Eden flowed the four great rivers that watered the earth. The paradox of depicting a paradise *on*, but not *of*, the earth presented a challenge to the mapmakers, who indicated the 'separate but connected' nature of paradise in various ways.

On the Hereford map, paradise is a walled garden on a remote island at the bounds of the earth (Fig 34). Eden was also portrayed as an oceanic island on the twelfth-century Sawley map (Fig 28). On maps in the various copies of Lambert of St Omer's *Liber Floridus* (written about 1120), an island paradise is further separated from the inhabited regions by an enclosure, appearing to indicate either a wall of fire or a ring of high mountains as described above (Fig 44). Another way of emphasising the isolation of paradise was by representing the Fall on the map. This had created the temporal barrier that prevented man from re-entering the garden from which he was banned, as shown on Beatus of Liébana's map discussed in the previous chapter (Figs 26 and 27). On all maps depicting its spatial isolation, paradise is connected to the inhabited regions of the earth through the four rivers.

The connection implied by the rivers is echoed in the relationship, emphasised in some maps, between centre and periphery, Eden and Jerusalem. Inaccessible, at the extremity of the earth, and at the limits of time and space, the earthly paradise stood for the act that had brought about man's fallen state. Yet it also pointed to the centre of the earth and to Jerusalem, the place of Christ's crucifixion and resurrection. On the thirteenth-century Psalter map, where Christ is shown dominating the world, as he does on the Hereford map (Fig 45), the observer's eye is drawn from the circle that contains the faces of Adam and Eve in paradise down the map, travelling westwards along the route of salvation history to another circle, that of the city of Jerusalem (Fig 46).

Fig 44 *World map, from a manuscript of Lambert of St Omer's* Liber Floridus *(c.1112–21), Belgium or northern France, third quarter of the twelfth century. Wolfenbüttel, Herzog August Bibliothek, Cod. Guelf. 1 Gud. lat., fols 69v–70r. The part reproduced here is the left side of the map, fol.69v, featuring the northern hemisphere with the inhabited earth and an equatorial paradise in the further east (at the top).*

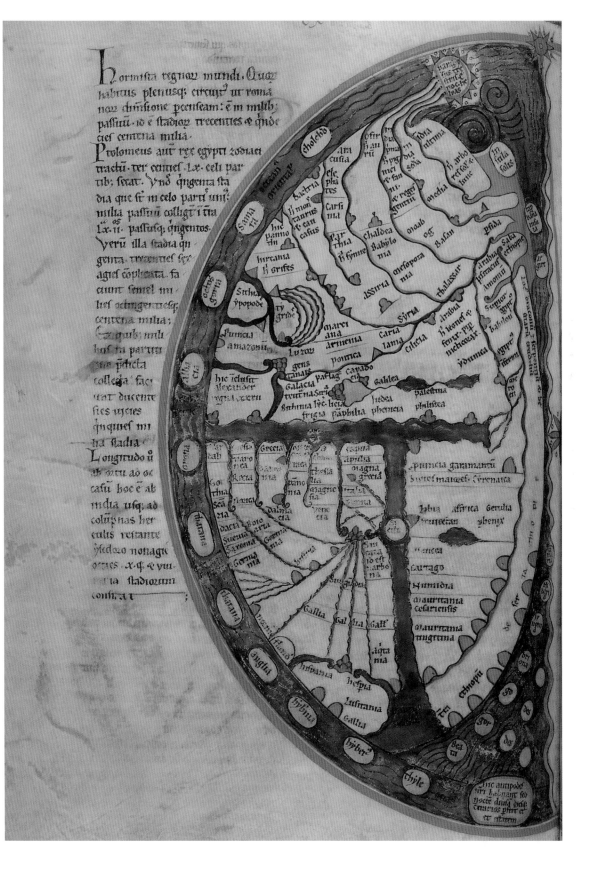

Hormista regnor mundi. Quor
habitus plenusq; circuit ut roma
nor christione peenseam: e in milib;
passuu. io e stadior trecenties e qude
cies centena milia.

Prolomeus aut rex egyti zodiaci
tractu. ter centies. lx. celi par
tib; secat. Vno qngenta sta
dia que si in celo parti uni?
milia passuu colligi i tia
lx. ii. passusq; qngentos.

verum illa stadia qn
genta trecenties fer
agies coplicata. fa
ciunt semel mi
lies octingentiesq;
centena milia;
Sriquis mili
bus in partiu
suo pdicta
colligat faci
uat ducentie
sies uicies
qnquies mi
lia stadia.

Longitudo ū
ab ortu ao oc
casu hoc e ab
india usq; ad
collipnas her
culis restante
ysedoro nonage
octies. x. q. e vni
na stadiozum
consuat;

Fig 45 (opposite) *The Psalter map. London, c.1265. London, British Library, Add. MS 28681, fol.9r.*

Fig 46 (above) *Detail of Fig 45: the earthly paradise and Jerusalem.*

Curiously, the medieval paradox of a paradise on earth seems to find an echo in modern quantum mechanics (dealing with physical phenomena at the sub-atomic scale – a branch of physics developed, among others, by Bohr, Heisenberg, Schrödinger and de Broglie). The realisation of the way in which sub-atomic matter does not exist with certainty at definite places, showing rather 'tendencies to exist' in various regions (always oscillating between different forms of existence) is reminiscent of the impossibility of pinpointing the exact location of the earthly paradise. The fact that paradise belonged to history, but was believed to exist still, somewhere in a virtual present, brings to mind the conversion, taking place within the atom, of the temporal sequence into a simultaneous co-existence of past, present and future. Also it is possible in our common experience to look back into the past: when we look at distant stars, we are seeing them as they were millions of years ago.

Moreover, in many medieval legends we learn of fortunate pilgrims experiencing the earthly paradise for only a brief instant, while on the outside many decades or several generations elapse in the human world. A physicist today would say that the Garden of Eden existed on earth, but in a time–space continuum of its own. In fact, according to modern physics, time flows at different rates in different parts of the universe, depending on the frame of reference of the observer. It seems a series of paradoxes belong to the intrinsic nature of paradise (and of sub-atomic reality), paradoxes that point to a unity of opposites to be found on a higher plane.

Furthermore it has become easier, since the advent of computer technology and the creation of animated cartography, to comprehend the medieval conception of a map of the world able to accommodate not only geographical space, but also historical time. This chapter opened with reference to *Google Earth* and the way this novelty allows a panoramic view of any point of earth at the time the images were recorded. In 2009 a technical refinement was introduced by the creators of *Google Earth* that allows the operator to move backwards and forwards in time on the screen. With *Historical Imagery*, panoramas from previous years can be selected and compared, environmental changes over time noted and the history of the contemporary world explored.

Modern virtual cartography is thus becoming as dynamic and interactive as the reality that it attempts to record. Today's priorities may differ from those of the Middle Ages, yet in a weird and rather unexpected manner modern mapping technology is echoing the medieval world-view that described a place from the past still existing, somehow, in the present. The idea of mapping time as well as space is no longer alien or exotic.

Visual Interlude
Paradise on the Ebstorf World Map

◆

The idea that the Garden of Eden was an 'event-place' at the very boundary of time and space provided the foundation for many renditions of the Garden of Eden on maps from the Middle Ages. On the Ebstorf world map, possibly made in Ebstorf in northern Germany, and variously dated between the early thirteenth and the beginning of the fourteenth century, the Garden of Eden is represented at the top of the map by a rectangle. Enclosed within it are Adam and Eve, the four rivers (shown disappearing into the ground), the Tree of Life and the Tree of the Knowledge of Good and Evil (Figs 47 and 48). As confirmed by a nearby inscription, Eden is the first region of Asia (starting from the Orient) and is surrounded by a wall of fire that reaches up to heaven. The four great rivers of the earth have their origin in paradise and, after flowing below the surface of the earth, they reappear in different regions.

The mysterious garden, surrounded on all sides by mountains, is located in the east, beyond India, near the outer ocean and near the head of a gigantic Christ, who is shown embracing the whole earth. The Greek letters alpha and omega appear on either side of Christ's head, together with the words 'Primus et novissimus' ('the first and the last'; Revelation 1.17). Christ's outstretched hands appear on either side of the earth, to the north and south. By his right hand, which is marked by the stigmata, is a quotation from Psalm 118.16: 'The right hand of the Lord doeth valiantly'. By his left hand we read: 'He holds the earth in his hand', a passage found in a liturgical text, the Antiphonary of the Office. His two feet are in the extreme west.

Fig 47 (opposite and overleaf) *The Ebstorf world map, ?Ebstorf, Lower Saxony, 1235–40 or c.1300. Facsimile in Kloster Ebstorf.*

Fig 48 (left) *Detail of Fig 47: the earthly paradise..*

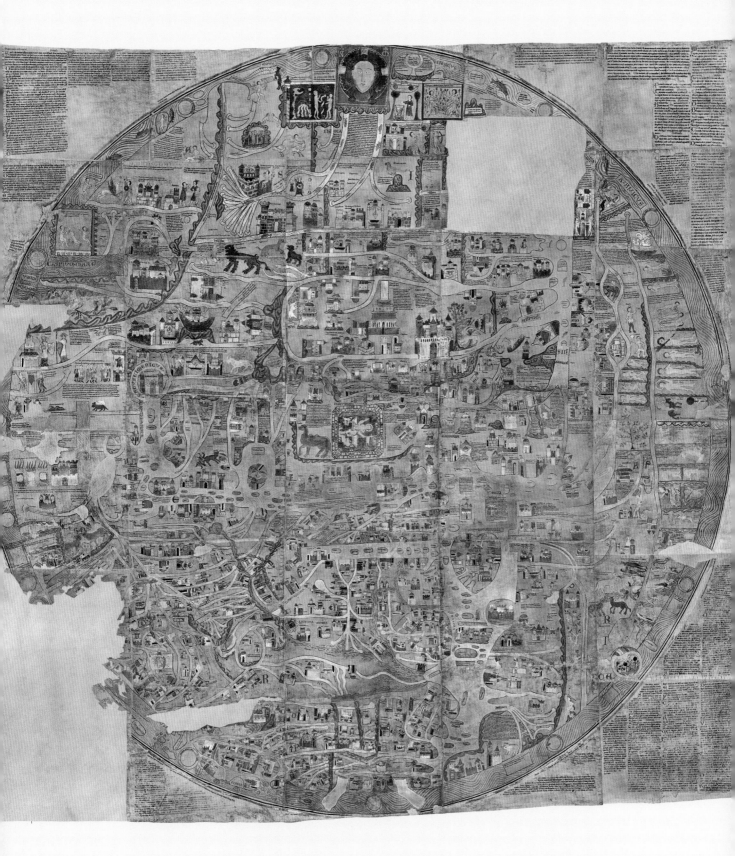

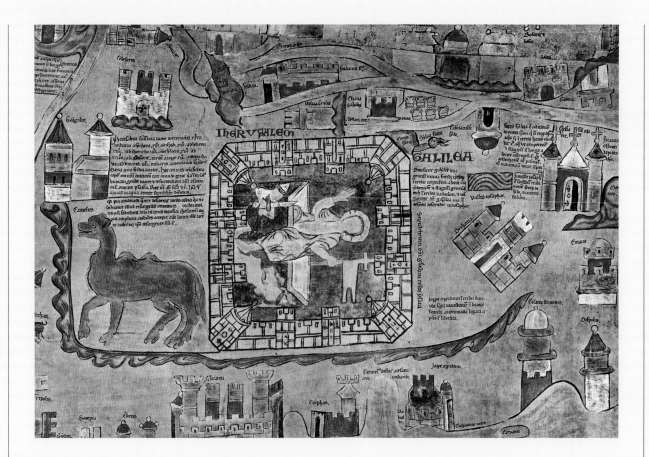

The quotation nearby reads 'Mightily to the end, sweetly ordering all things', and is inspired by the Book of Wisdom 8.1.

The Wisdom of God, Christ himself, as Saint Paul had made clear (1 Corinthians 1.24), extended from the beginning to the end of the world. Christ's global embrace points to the way God has structured salvation history between Adam's Fall and the advent of his son. From paradise in the east, featuring original sin, the course of history leads the observer's eye down the map to its central point, Jerusalem. The city is dominated by the figure of Christ rising from the grave, signifying Jerusalem's role as the meeting point of heaven and earth (Fig 49).

In honour of the special status of the historical and earthly Jerusalem, where the resurrection of Christ inaugurated the wait for the end of time, the city is depicted on the map with gilded walls

Fig 49 *Detail of Fig 47: Jerusalem and the Holy Land.*

and 12 gates – as described in the apocalyptic account of the Heavenly Jerusalem given in the Book of Revelation (chapters 21.11–12, 16, 18). The two-humped camel, besides indicating the presence of camels in Palestine, may also refer to the humility of Christ, who lowered himself, as the camel does, to take on the burden of human weakness. Alternatively, it may have been intended to underline the glory of a Jerusalem that is open to all nations and thus accessible to multitudes of camels from everywhere, as celebrated by the prophet Isaiah (60.6).

Bibliographic Essay

———— ◆ ————

Many studies in the history of cartography have highlighted the capacity of medieval *mappae mundi* to blend time and space: see, for example, Evelyn Edson, *Mapping Time and Space: How Medieval Mapmakers Viewed Their World* (London: The British Library, 1997).

Historians of cartography such as Peter Barber, Catherine Delano-Smith and Roger Kain, Patrick Gautier Dalché, Paul Harvey and David Woodward have pointed out that mathematical exactitude was not the object of medieval *mappae mundi*. Modern historians of cartography have abandoned the simplistic vision of a linear progression to recognise that the corpus of medieval maps represents an alternative cartographical system, and have attacked the pretence that cartography can attain a scientific and objective *non plus ultra* in the representation of the world. They have commented on the inherent subjectivity of maps and the dangers of viewing cartography as an objective activity: see, for example, J. B. Harley, *The New Nature of Maps. Essays in the History of Cartography*, Paul Laxton, ed. (Baltimore and London: The Johns Hopkins Press, 2001), and Denis Cosgrove's Introduction to *Mappings* (London: Reaktion Books, 1999). The myth that cartographical methods reflect, in J. B. Harley's words, the 'cumulative progress of an objective science always producing better delineations of reality' ('Deconstructing the Map', *Cartographica*, 26:2 (1989), p.15), has been rejected not only by historians of cartography, but also by modern practising cartographers (see, for example, Alan M. MacEachren, *How Maps Work: Representation, Visualization, and Design* (New York–London: The Guilford Press, 1995).

On Hugh of Saint Victor, see Roger Baron, *Études sur Hugues de Saint-Victor* (Paris: Desclée de Brouwer, 1963); Joachim Ehlers, *Hugo von St Viktor. Studien zum Geschichtsdenken und zur Geschichtsschreibung des 12. Jahrhunderts* (Wiesbaden: Steiner Werlag, 1973); Patrick Gautier Dalché, *La 'Descriptio Mappe Mundi'*

de Hugues de Saint-Victor (Paris: Études Augustiniennes, 1988); Patrice Sicard, *Diagrammes médiévaux et exégèse visuelle: le* Libellus de formatione arche *de Hugues de Saint-Victor* (Paris-Turnhout: Brepols, 1993); Dominique Poirel, *Hugues de Saint-Victor* (Paris: Cerf, 1998). Hugh explained his vision of history and geography, for example, in his *De Archa Noe*, IV.9, Patrice Sicard, ed., *Corpus Christianorum, Continuatio Medievalis* CLXXVI (Turnhout: Brepols, 2001), pp.111–12.

A number of *mappae mundi* are discussed in Peter Barber, ed., *The Map Book* (London: Weidenfeld and Nicolson, 2005). On the Hereford Map, see P. D. A. Harvey, ed., *The Hereford World Map: Medieval World Maps and Their Context* (London: The British Library, 2006); Scott D. Westrem, *The Hereford Map. A Transcription and Translation of the Legends with Commentary* (Turnhout: Brepols, 2001); Naomi R. Kline, *Maps of Medieval Thought* (Woodbridge: The Boydell Press, 2001); P. D. A. Harvey, *Mappa Mundi: the Hereford World Map* (London: Hereford Cathedral–The British Library; Toronto: University of Toronto Press, 1996). On the Ebstorf map, destroyed during Second World War and now only available as a pre-war facsimile, there is an abundant literature, mostly in German; for the most recent reproduction, transcription and commentary see Hartmut Kugler, ed., *Die Ebstorfer Weltkarte* (Berlin: Akademie Verlag, 2007), and Armin Wolf, 'The Ebstorf *Mappamundi* and Gervase of Tilbury: The Controversy Revisited', *Imago Mundi*, 64/1, 2012, pp.1–27. Austrian-born American physicist Fritjof Capra has explored the parallels between modern physics and eastern mysticism in his *The Tao of Physics* (London: Flamingo, 1982). For a recent survey on modern theories of space–time, see Luciano Boi, 'Theories of Space–Time in Modern Physics', in Thomas Baldwin, ed., *The Cambridge History of Philosophy, 1870–1945* (Cambridge: Cambridge University Press, 2003), pp.207–18.

CHAPTER 5

WHERE IS NOWHERE?

*This estuary is huge. The water has changed from salt to fresh. I have never
read or heard of so great a quantity of fresh water coming into the sea. Where is
all this water coming from? From far away, perhaps, and it collects here, to form
this kind of lake. The climate is mild. The indigenous people around here are
handsome, intelligent and brave as well as peaceful and friendly.
All these signs agree with the opinion of our holy and wise theologians,
and I wonder if I am close to the earthly paradise...*

FROM CHRISTOPHER COLUMBUS'S
JOURNAL OF HIS THIRD VOYAGE TO
THE NEW WORLD, 1498

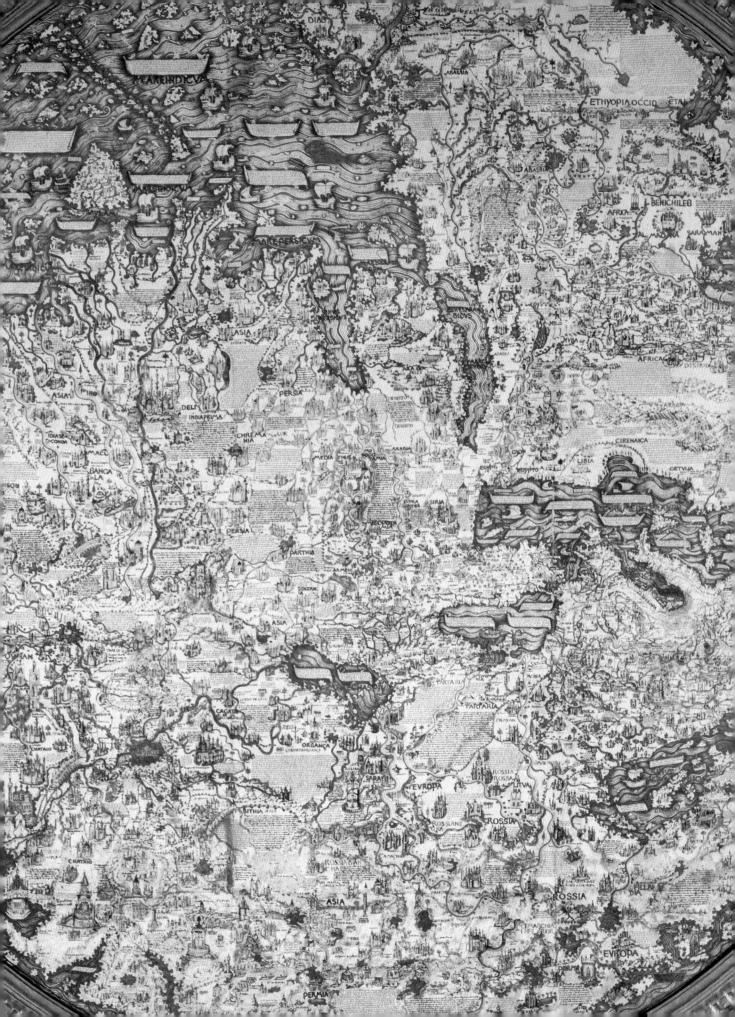

GLIMPSING PARADISE FROM A DISTANCE

In 1498 Christopher Columbus reached the South American mainland. Having sailed west across the ocean for several months, he believed himself to be near Asia's easternmost part, thinking that Asia was only a few thousand nautical miles to the west of Europe. As he entered the estuary of the River Orinoco, Columbus was overwhelmed by the sight of a great watery expanse. Wonders multiplied around him. He felt that his caravel was sailing upward, not horizontally. He speculated that the earth was not perfectly round, contrary to the opinions of astrologers and philosophers, but had a protuberance, like a pear which is round except where the stalk grows. It seemed possible to him that on this protrusion, similar in shape also to a woman's nipple, the earthly paradise was to be found.

Perhaps – Columbus wrote down in his journal – he was sailing up to the highest mountain on earth, situated at the equator and at the extremity of the ocean. Perhaps the mass of fresh water that he was encountering issued from the top of that mountain, and originated in paradise. Certainly he did not entertain any hope that he himself could enter the Garden of Eden. To Columbus the earthly paradise was known to be inaccessible and beyond the horizon for ordinary humans. Very likely, he may have thought, the stream leading to the summit of that extreme protuberance was not navigable. Undoubtedly, he wrote in his journal, ascent was not possible because no man could enter the earthly paradise.

Columbus might have sensed the proximity of paradise, but he did not believe that he was on its very threshold. For him, the mystery that paradise could be simultaneously present on earth and also in the beyond was sufficient in itself. The situation is not so different today, when most of us have little difficulty in accepting the idea that remote and unreachable galaxies exist in deepest space. Throughout the Middle Ages and into the Renaissance, Christian belief in an earthly paradise rested on the inherent duality of the place: its separateness and (through the four rivers) connectedness with the inhabited earth. This is the paradox that provides the key to the presence of an earthly paradise on medieval maps of the world. The Garden of Eden was located at the head of the river of time as well as in an inaccessible eastern location, and no physical journey could ever allow the return to the original innocence.

In the late fifteenth century Columbus still lived in a mental universe that Dante, the Italian poet of the fourteenth century, would have recognised. In his *Divine Comedy*, a literary account of his journey through the three realms of the other world (hell, purgatory and heaven), Dante meets the Greek hero Ulysses, or Odysseus, in hell. Here the latter endures eternal punishment for the fraudulent stratagem of the Wooden Horse, by means of which the city of Troy was taken. Ulysses tells Dante that after the capture of Troy he persuaded his companions to sail to the unknown further than the Pillars of Hercules, beyond which, for the classical world, no man was permitted to venture. They left Gibraltar for the Atlantic, on a southwesterly course. After five months at sea the Greek hero caught sight of the high mountain of

Previous page: *World map by Fra Mauro. Venice, c.1450. Venice, Biblioteca Nazionale Marciana. Detail of Fig 59: parts of Europe, Asia and Africa.*

Fig 50 (opposite) Il globo terracqueo secondo l'Alighieri, *from Edoardo Coli*, Il paradiso terrestre dantesco *(Florence: Carnesecchi, 1897), fig 22. London, British Library, Ac.8848.*

paradise in the distance; but his ship was immediately overwhelmed by a storm, for no living human was allowed to complete the crossing of that sea and reach paradise on earth: for Dante, the ascent of that mountain was the purifying journey of human souls to recover the life of Eden. The exceptionally high mountain of paradise that bordered on heaven was kept separate from the inhabited regions of the earth by an impassable ocean (Fig 50). Ulysses's journey, in Dante's words, was a *folle volo*, a 'mad flight', because man on his own, lacking the support of divine revelation, is not allowed to penetrate the mystery of the earthly paradise.

It was not only Ulysses's vessel that was wrecked within sight of the mountain-island that was crowned by paradise. In the thirteenth century, medieval scholars such as Roger Bacon and St Albert the Great tried enthusiastically to unlock the mystery of its location, but their efforts too were doomed to eventual failure.

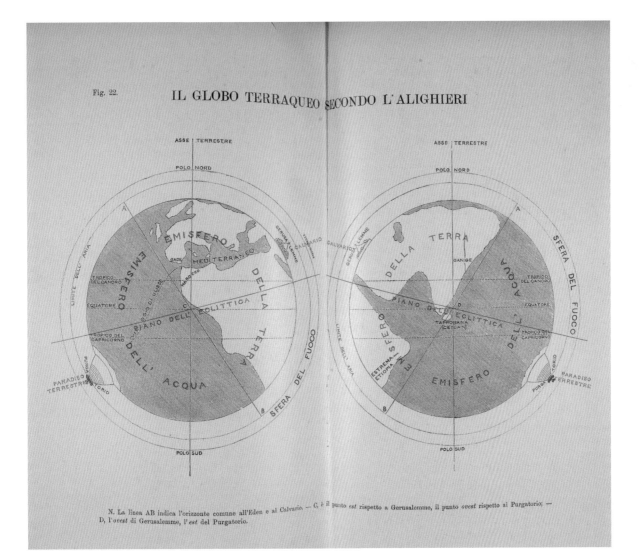

Fig. 22.

IL GLOBO TERRAQUEO SECONDO L'ALIGHIERI

N. La linea AB indica l'orizzonte comune all'Eden e al Calvario. — C, è il punto *est* rispetto a Gerusalemme, il punto *ovest* rispetto al Purgatorio; — D, l'*ovest* di Gerusalemme, l'*est* del Purgatorio.

GRASPING THE MYSTERY

Once thirteenth-century Western Christian scholars tried to unravel the geographical contradictions of a paradise on earth, they found they had set themselves an uphill task. The Christian notion of an earthly paradise was essentially a paradox, implying as it did a heavenly locality on earth, different from the rest of this world and escaping 'normal' natural conditions, yet part of real geography. In paradise there were no seasons: it was eternally spring, fruit and flowers never faded or failed and the harvest was plentiful all the year around. But where on earth was such a delightful and perfectly temperate place to be found?

The Old Latin version (the *Vetus Latina*), circulating in the early centuries of Christianity, had explained that paradise had been planted 'in the east'. Such location was confirmed by Isidore of Seville in the seventh, Bede in the eighth, the unnamed compilers of the *Glossa ordinaria* and the commentator Peter Lombard in the twelfth century. Paradise had been named by these scholars as *somewhere* in eastern Asia, but none of them had ventured to suggest exactly where. In the thirteenth century, however, the problem of the terrestrial paradise's location assumed greater importance in the context of the revival of astronomical geography – part of the overall intellectual revolution produced by the introduction to the West of the new learning derived from Aristotle and his Arab commentators. Theologians had to account for the Christian belief in an earthly paradise in the light of new geographical and astronomical data, and they embraced the challenge.

The idea of parallel zones, beginning from the equator and going towards the poles, reached scholars in the Middle Ages through Greek mathematical and astronomical geography. The region near the equator, called the torrid zone, and the polar circles were considered equally uninhabitable due to either excessive heat or cold. The region known from experience to be inhabited was the temperate area in the northern hemisphere. Controversy, however, surrounded the equatorial region and the whole of the southern hemisphere, and the problem of the earthly paradise's location was linked to the debate over their habitability. One idea that emerged from the interest in the division of the globe into different parts, for example, was a belief that the fiery sword of the biblical Cherubim guarding the entrance to the Garden of Eden could be a reference to the torrid zone, traditionally regarded as impassable because of excessive heat, with the earthly paradise lying beyond it. So, if few scholars suggested that the eastern paradise was in an unknown region in the northern hemisphere, the general tendency was to situate it either on the equator or south of the equator, beyond the torrid zone.

Aristotle's idea that the equatorial zone was too hot for human habitation was contradicted by other ancient Greek thinkers, such as Ptolemy, and by more recent Muslim scholars such as Avicenna. It was also disproved by Arabic astronomical tables, which indicated that in fact a number of cities were to be found along the equator. Following these beliefs, some medieval scholars, such as Alexander of Hales, Robert Grosseteste and Robertus Anglicus, thought that the lands at the equator were not only temperate and habitable, but also the best place for life. They thus placed paradise there.

Others continued to hold Aristotle's opinion that the equator was uninhabitable. They favoured the idea of zonal symmetry, which meant an uninhabitable middle (equatorial) zone, but accommodated the possibility of human life in an antipodean temperate zone, inaccessible because of the intervening torrid zone. Excluding, for theological reasons, the possibility of inhabitants in the Antipodes (which would contradict the unity of the human race and of salvation history), several Christian authors argued that since the southern hemisphere would not have been created for no purpose, it must accommodate the earthly paradise. The idea was put forward, for example, by one of the commentators of the *Tractatus de sphera* of Iohannes de Sacrobosco (an outstandingly influential work of astronomical geography in the Middle Ages), possibly Michael Scot.

Late medieval scholars failed to reach a consensus, and the question of whether paradise was located at the equator, or south of the equator, remained an ongoing issue up to the Renaissance. The continuing uncertainty is seen in, for example, the writings of St Albert the Great, who initially believed that Eden was in the southern hemisphere (in his *Summa de creaturis*, 1246), then changed his mind and claimed that it was at the equator (in his commentary on Peter Lombard's *Sentences*, 1249), and finally avoided the topic altogether (in his *De natura locorum*, *c*.1260, and in his final work, the *Summa theologiae*, written after 1270). Albert's pupil St Thomas Aquinas, who also speculated about the various possible locations of the Garden of Eden, took no position. Roger Bacon, who insisted that theologians interpreting the paradise narrative in Genesis needed a sound mathematical, geographical and astronomical knowledge, avoided endorsing any of the opinions he systematically discussed in his *Opus maius* (1267), and gave no hint of a definitive conclusion as to the precise location of paradise. Any attempt to express the paradise question in purely rational and physical terms, or to pin paradise down to a recognisable geographical location, was doomed to failure. Eventually, deprived of its aura of mystery by being dissected as a topographical feature, the Garden of Eden was to prove to be in an inaccessible *nowhere*.

PARADISE AND THE CLIMATIC ZONES

The whole of the thirteenth century was spent in lengthy scholarly debate on how to reconcile the location of the earthly paradise with the astronomical division of the globe. East-orientated and historical *mappae mundi* were not the only kind of map showing the world and circulating in the West throughout the Latin Middle Ages. Zonal maps – diagrammatic maps showing the sequence of five climatic belts encircling the earth as defined in classical times (two frigid, two temperate and one torrid zone along the equator) – were drawn to illustrate medieval copies of the ancient geographical texts. Unlike east-orientated *mappae mundi*, zonal maps were usually orientated to the south or north (Fig 51). Also unlike *mappae mundi*, which portrayed the inhabited northern hemisphere as adjacent to paradise and on which history was the overriding factor, the zonal map depicted the whole terrestrial globe in an entirely ahistorical manner, showing the earth divided into zones determined through astronomical observation. Both *mappae mundi* and zonal maps were part of Christian medieval culture, but the vast majority of zonal maps lack any map sign for paradise. There is nothing surprising in this. A zonal map of the earth was by definition focused on the physical structure of the globe – its division into climatic zones – and not on the development of humankind's history in earthly space. The zonal map served a purpose – the definition of climatic zones – that was inconsistent with the inclusion of the Garden of Eden.

However, paradise was occasionally included on a zonal map by inserting a simplified *mappa mundi* on to the zonal configuration – as, for example, in a map penned on a folio at the end of a twelfth-century Bible from Arnstein, Germany (Fig 52). This map is east-orientated, and the zones run vertically down the page. Paradise is marked at the top of the northern hemisphere, where a detailed depiction is presented. In this way, a historical dimension was introduced into a spatial representation ruled otherwise only by the astronomical zones of classical science. Indeed, a contradiction is inherent in conflating two cartographical genres based on quite different principles.

How was it possible to associate paradise with any of the world's climatic zones? There were zones known as 'temperate' in both the northern and the southern hemispheres, but they were supposed to be subject to changing atmospheric conditions. Not only was the location of paradise unknown, but, with its perpetually temperate weather, paradise fitted none of the climatic belts. Paradise had to be some quite special area independent from 'normal' weather conditions.

One map, found in a late twelfth-century copy of the *Navigatio Sancti Brendani*, accommodates paradise in another zonal depiction with remarkable ingenuity and demonstrates in a striking manner the way in which the Garden of Eden was believed simultaneously to exist on earth and yet to be in a 'different' region outside the inhabited earth and outside its climatic divisions (Fig 53). The Brendan map, as it has been called, is oriented to the south and is a representation of the terrestrial sphere, which shows the five climatic zones. A circle represents the inhabited earth, with its southern and northern boundaries, named

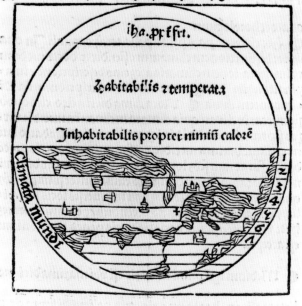

Fig 51 (below) *Zonal world map with climates, from Iohannes de Sacrobosco,* Tractatus de sphere *(Leipzig: Martinus Landsberg, ?1495), sig.fvii v. London, British Library, IA.11977.*

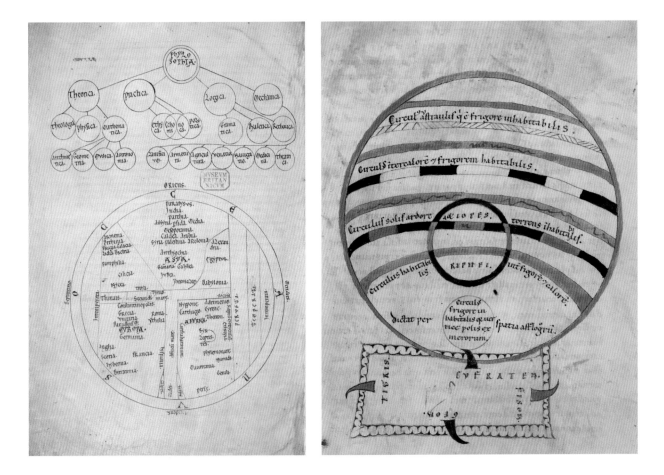

Fig 52 (above left) *World map, from the Arnstein Bible, Arnstein, Germany, 1172. London, British Library, MS Harley 2799, fol.241v.*

Fig 53 (above right) *The 'Brendan map', southern Germany, late twelfth century. Bischofszell (Canton of Thurgovia, Switzerland), Ortsmuseum, Dr Albert Knoepfli Stiftung.*

Aetiopes and *Riphei* respectively. Paradise is represented by a large rectangle drawn below the terrestrial globe. The rectangle appears to touch the spherical globe, but it is shown on a different plane to emphasise the separateness of paradise from the earth and its climatic division. Only the four rivers of paradise, indicated and named on the rectangle, connect the two otherwise unconnectable planes.

The two cartographical discourses, that of the historical *mappa mundi* and that of the astronomical zonal map, were on different planes, as it were, and essentially incompatible. It was theoretically impossible to show the earthly paradise on a map structured on astronomical measurements. The relatively uncommon hybrid zonal–historical maps, however, reflect how geography was beginning to catch up with history in the later Middle Ages. Paradise on a zonal map was a geographical statement, suggesting a specific location associated with global space measured through astronomical observation and divided into climatic zones – quite unlike the historical, but geographically rather vague, intimation of paradise on a *mappa mundi*.

RETURN TO THE BIBLE

Up to the fourteenth century theologians had been trying to harmonise Christian faith with the contemporary scientific world view without betraying the Church's traditions. Thereafter, however, they were obliged by the wide range of paradoxes and problems involved in the attempt to locate the Garden of Eden on earth to abandon a rational approach to the paradise question and to give up trying to define their faith in terms of Aristotelian science and mathematical astronomy. Fourteenth-century scholars tended to shy away from the range of scientific requirements based on the geographical debate by placing paradise at as great a distance as possible from the earth, situated on a high mountain, and thus isolated from conditions in the climatic zone at its base.

As attempts to explain the location of paradise through science continued to decline, exegetes turned back to the Bible. The fourteenth-century French Franciscan Nicholas of Lyre, for example, rigorously avoided any speculation not based on the words on the written page. Whereas scholars in the thirteenth century, such as Roger Bacon, had believed that mathematical astronomy was essential for the understanding of the Scriptures, Nicholas maintained that theology was superior to all other sciences and that the Bible, which surpassed all other writings, was the only real text for theologians. While Nicholas had to admit that the location of the earthly paradise remained uncertain, he also insisted that divine revelation coming from Scripture should be accepted by faith and not by reason.

The earlier trend to interpret the religious mystery of paradise in terms of rational geography was reversed. In the early fourteenth century John Duns Scotus placed great emphasis on the impossibility of discovering the location of the Garden of Eden and on the miraculous aspect of its geography. In his view, without God's aid, human intelligence was incapable of grasping the mystery of paradise – something that could be approached only through faith and by bowing to the authority of the Bible. For him it was not at all surprising that the earthly paradise eluded all rational attempts to locate it; faith alone would bridge the gulf between human knowledge and God's plan as revealed in Holy Scripture.

GEOGRAPHY CATCHES UP ON MAPS

By the beginning of the fifteenth century, the exegetical stage was set for crucial changes in how paradise was conceived. There were also major changes in cartography. A new conceptual framework was developing in the field of mapmaking, heralded by the occasional merging of the astronomical zonal maps and the historical *mappae mundi*. The appearance in the world of navigation of the nautical chart, possibly around 1200, introduced a completely different cartographical mindset, which by the end of the fifteenth century had radically changed European mapping.

Nautical charts were made for practical use. They were used to guide navigation within the enclosed or nearly enclosed waters of the Mediterranean and Black Seas (or perhaps to show the navigational skill of their owners), and, as Mediterranean sailors ventured with increasing regularity into the Atlantic, along the oceanic shores of Europe and Africa. The charts portrayed these coastlines with remarkable accuracy, together with the names of major ports and prominent coastal features. Ruled lines, known as rhumbs, radiated from wind roses (which indicated on the map the cardinal directions) to provide the means of working out the shortest compass course between different places. It seems that charts had sometimes been used in the fourteenth century in the compilation of *mappae mundi*, as indicated by the delineation of the Mediterranean coastline. The earliest known world maps to show the influence of a nautical chart in this way are thought to be those constructed about 1320 by Pietro Vesconte (Fig 54). A later example is provided by the Leardo map discussed in chapter 2.

The transfer of the Mediterranean coastline from nautical chart to world map implied far more than cartographical refinement. It intimated a radically different approach to the representation of space, as measurable distance and direction were essential for a sailor who needed to work out his route from the map. The insertion of coastal outlines prepared for navigation or to celebrate the skill of sailors into a historically structured *mappa mundi* announced a critical break. Henceforth space was perceived differently, and the mapping of the world became a matter of increasingly accurate measurement of angles and directions and, eventually, distance. The plotting of places according to contiguity, that is without taking into account their measured interrelationship, was losing ground as a way of representing the world cartographically.

Before the fourteenth century, many world maps had been essentially historical representations, referring to the past and only partially mirroring contemporary features inasmuch as these related to the present state of the Christian world. Their portrayal of lands in southern Africa and eastern Asia had been taken mainly from ancient sources. At the beginning of the fifteenth century, however, maritime cartography offered the compilers of *mappae mundi* an alternative perspective: to represent the Asian and African parts of the known world as contemporary and not historical. Contemporary information could be taken from Arabic maps and geographical tables and, above all, from European travellers' accounts. A flood of new information about distant parts of the world, most especially about Asia and its eastern extremities, had reached Western Europe and altered the way in which such regions were perceived and portrayed on maps. Fifteenth-century mapmakers were encouraged by the reports reaching them to portray non-European lands as regions of the present, not of the past – and thus no longer purely as the stage for a display of Christian universal history. Moreover, the centre of gravity of book and map production had shifted away from the predominantly rural monastic *scriptoria* to the university towns and mercantile cities.

The traditional intimate connection between the historical dimension and geographical description was gradually being lost. Not by chance, a number of world maps produced in the fifteenth century were oriented in a variety of ways, having

Fig 54 (overleaf) *World map attributed to Pietro Vesconte, from Marino Sanudo,* Liber secretorum fidelium crucis super Terrae Sanctae recuperatione et conservatione, *Genoa or Venice, c.1325. London, British Library, Add. MS 27376, fols.187v–188r.*

Parcia ab occre ht idus siu, a midie mare in dias ab rubz abocante media, a sept yr
tein fines uirare oñe origine excruerie, fuere ei ceules q pu sonar attica lingua, ah uir yralaz
Inoia medis eñi sur guindecs, in ea e siria media q psia. Assyria dea ab asiur, ab oñente ht
a sept anustia. Est aiie caucañe mos qui a caspio man oriens attolli, et p aquilee ñgh
prue ust ad europa springitur et pgetai ac linguar uariente idiussis siu prb, ditus...
mote noiatur, ubi eum diuerse excresso, e primu eu catoie, caucasus di albi di isan
tus, alibi serapedon, alibi por caspiu, alibi miranus, alibi corasie, alibi siregis
gete cola sarmate. In radia caucast supauit alecanter piancas euergetos
pauimas parpamenos adalpios cetrosq ipsos. Media dea a medo re
ge ab oñente caspios uidicit, a mendie pisdam, ab occai triusa piie re
gna amplecti, a sept armeis dcidatur. In una parte bitui saricem
in alia noeat cordiue. Est aut duplex media maior et minor, Psia
a p seo rege qui ex greta transir, ab oñente tendit ust ad idos
occau rubiu mare ab aquilone mediam. Sitia sic et gotia a
magog silio Japhet cognominata, a texra oñentis parte ua
oceanus senais est, extendiatur usq ad mare caspium, qd
est adociasum, a mendie uo de hinc usq ad caucasum, et
et subia occ ei uirania. Yrcania ab oñente mare cas
pium a mendie armeniam, ab occidente ybernia post
quam capadocia ab aquilone albania, ab yrania
gascantur cine hec ab oñente sub mari caspio co
gurgens per ozan occeana septemtrionalis ad me
oñdas paludes p deserta extenditur.

Egus qui ali intre he alre parti
dell Asia

europa a fluuio tanay usq ad fines yspaie
engiatur et in insula guides uel melius in
pit sc uin oñtay de regno spraigalis fini
ñce infrascriptas prouidas. Sichia inte
a meondis paludibus ust gmaia po
guar, q ist babaros iluitrus babaica di gan
alania pite par q ad meondes palures pañ
st hec dana ii q gotia. Germaia pt siua ab
he ht danubi a midie unu istior. Mel
ab oñente boshis danuby claudiatur, a mi
q macedonie, ab occau ystrie iungit, a sept da
bus douides a barbaro ii siit uadali iugi
lit turnligi uinuli qui postea ytalia posseder
gogobadi di sur, scowobruni scoringi mauigi go
noi aspia bulgares q buni a eragoza di sur
gilanoi grepia samare siueu panoni q ist yralia
endur saxones nona qui q baioary q ab oñente
it panoia ab occau suema a midie ytalia a sept
inubu. Diuna ab oñte ht ostantinopli a midie
eu mari a sept ystria obtediatur. Grecia oli deu du ce
i sm bonu q ulie gnalr omis grecia e vii i septos oñu
prouitas. Dalmatia e ab oñte hus ab oñte macedoiaz
inoie mari adriaci ab occau ystra a sept messia. Epyrus
sata ab epyro achilis silio, aui po caronia q an molosia dea e
ides noiatu a rege elena media int macedoiaz q achaia ar
oie, a sept iugitur. Eladis due siit priue beoria q qua tixbe
prisia. Thesalia a mendie macedonie oñeta e au pina a typē
ea e mos pnasius odam apilnu coseratus. Macedonia ab oñete
et egro mari a mendie achaye ab occau dalmatie a sept messie
baia, tune insule e a sept oñi macedie iugit ul meli iugitur ducatu
enaz qui simu sire alua pribus maribs ariidatur, e, ab oñtu, midie u
opas insule, ht eapud coninthus archadia sinus e achaye in ion, q egream
ceuente ht mirtuum mare ab euro artenia pro magna pte iacet seas mare
eeidit ipa est sinonia. Panouia alpibus apennis ab ytalia secernatur ab
oñente hus messiam ab euro ystriam ab asnco motes apennos alps ab occau gu
brigicam, a sept slamen quod galiam et Germaniam diuidit, a mendie ytalie
inga a mendie prisa pyrine abocau...

Map labels

Albania · hic sit ma
gni miðie · mores caspie · Yrcania · oceanus · Georgia · colcia · Regio Zinbable
algozem · Tanay · Cumania · Panduha · Rutenia · Polonia · cracouia · letouni pagani
moraia · boemia · mistria · marchia · fideles pomonia · vngaria · Danubu · messia · stabula
Macedonia · Grecia · clados · Sclia · croatia · dalmatia · Istria · forum iulii · Anglia · Scotia · Ybernia · Germaia · Gallia · Nortugia · Iucia · viena · francia

hõ iudig

nebile

insula piperie

hic huit mlctudo tartaro

afiga

brelit

Indus fluui

India mag

India pua que et ethiopia

tra euftrates

arabia mecha si nichitur smaragdi

mare rubium

puintia oburge lya ethiopia iflor

bedoin

hadon   noge

chuo

habesse tin nigror

nubie

egyptus

na tyrenefis

Pentapolis

aramania

Regio inhitablis ip caloie

Sethiopia barban

syrtes maioes

locessim

Getulia

Gaulolia Regio vif montiu

Siroccus

Auster

south, north or west at the top rather than east, as mapmakers began to follow different cartographical traditions. This marked a crucial break with the practice of creating maps to communicate the east–west progression of history. The historico-geographical comprehensiveness offered by cartography was being reduced to the purely geographical and contemporary dimension. Yet paradise continued to be shown on the new maps, although now in a very different cartographical context.

Significantly, while some fifteenth-century mapmakers abandoned the traditional eastern orientation but continued to show an Asian paradise on their world maps (for example, on the Walsperger map, Fig 55), others preferred to change the location of the Garden of Eden entirely. They chose to place Eden instead in Africa, a sign that

Fig 55 (left) *World map by Andreas Walsperger, Constance, southern Germany, 1448. Vatican City, Biblioteca Apostolica Vaticana, MS Pal. Lat. 1362b, unfoliated.*

Fig 56 (above) *The Catalan Estense world map, ?Majorca, c.1450–60. Modena, Biblioteca Estense, C.G.A. 1.*

the primary concern had switched from showing the east–west succession of event-places of human history to the mapping of contemporary geographical space. The author of the so-called Catalan Estense world map of the 1450s (with north at the top) depicted Eden in the Horn of Africa, along the equator (Figs 56 and 57).

There were various factors to take into account in connection with an African paradise. By the fifteenth century Asia had been increasingly explored by Europeans, while central and southern Africa had remained largely unknown territory. St Jerome's Vulgate translation had implied that paradise had been planted 'in the beginning', not necessarily 'in the east'. 'East', anyway, was a relative notion that depended on the position of the observer, as John Duns Scotus had argued in the fourteenth century; thus a place 'in the east' could be anywhere, not necessarily, or only, in eastern Asia. The Nile, long believed to be one of the rivers of paradise (the Gihon), was known to flow through Africa, and the land of Cush, described in Genesis as being encircled by the Gihon, had been identified in Jerome's text with Ethiopia – a country long perceived as almost celestial, described by Marco Polo as a magnificent Christian land, and considered part of the same vast and mysterious region of India, the Ethiopians being often called Indians. The two lands mentioned in Genesis as neighbouring paradise, Havilah/India and Cush/Ethiopia, had in fact already been closely associated in the Graeco-Roman geographical tradition. From late antiquity on, various texts explicitly associated paradise and its rivers with Ethiopia. At the beginning of the sixth century, for example, Cesarius of Arles reported that, in order to reach paradise in Asia, someone had attempted the journey in Egypt, by following the course of the Nile upstream. He had failed because of the excessive heat at the equator.

Finally, a southern paradise had not been an entirely new idea in the fifteenth century. As early as the thirteenth century, some scholars (for example St Bonaventure, Roger Bacon and St Albert the Great) all seem in their different ways to have taken the idea of a paradise in the southern hempisphere very seriously. St Thomas Aquinas, too, had admitted the possibility that paradise could lie on, or beyond, the torrid zone.

We should always bear in mind, however, that by definition paradise lies outside the inhabited and known world. The choice of an African or Asian location for paradise means only that the African or Asian regions known to man were considered to border that *inaccessible* 'beyond'. Paradise was not

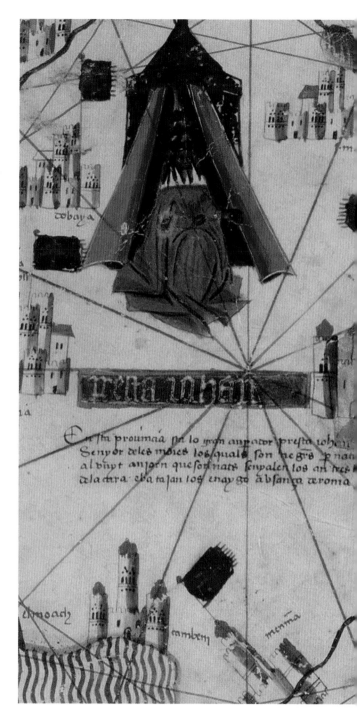

Fig 57 *Detail of Fig 56: the earthly paradise.*

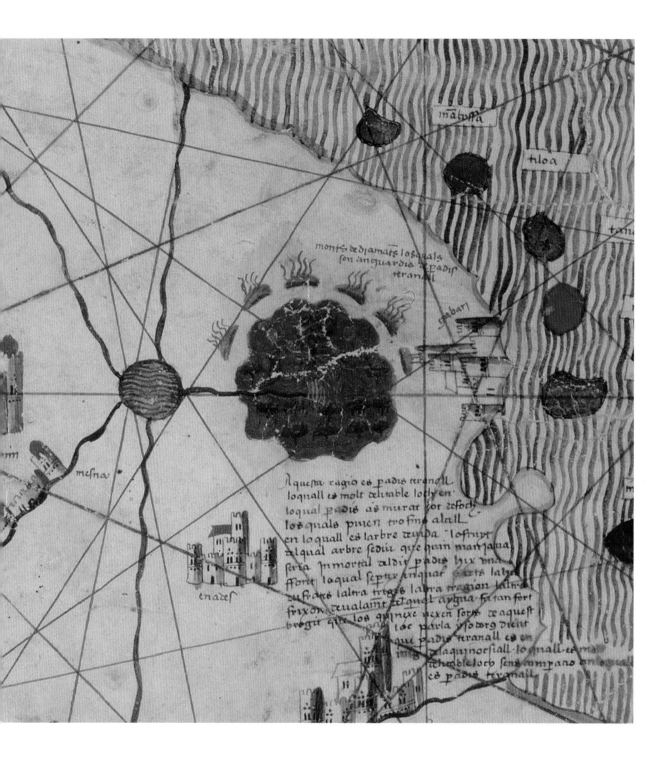

thought to be in Ethiopia (or in India), but *near* Ethiopia (or *near* India). Nobody could claim to know its exact location. Whatever region was thought to be bordering Eden, the downplaying of the historical dimension and the new concern with geographical accuracy made the inclusion of paradise on fifteenth-century maps even more problematic than before.

Visual Interlude
Paradise on Fra Mauro's World Map

◆

Fifteenth-century mapmakers faced the difficulty of having to find room for paradise, an unlocatable event-place, on maps that featured plottable and contemporary places and had lost the structural east–west progression of universal history. Fra Mauro, a Venetian monk in the Camaldolese monastery of San Michele on the island of Murano, found a brilliant solution, true to medieval tradition. He depicted the Garden of Eden in one of the four corner spaces left between the circular map of the inhabited earth and its square frame (Figs 58 and 59).

Fra Mauro's intention was to map the regions of his own day, not to chart the process of humankind's history. Thus in the main circle of his map, dated to about 1450, he showed the contemporary, inhabited earth in considerable detail. Around it, in the four corners of the square frame, he placed supplementary diagrams and texts to provide the wider context, illustrating the earth's relationship with the heavenly spheres and astral bodies and discussing what was believed to lie on the terrestrial globe beyond the inhabited and known regions. Both a text and a vignette make the point that paradise is situated far from the inhabited earth, in some unknown region of the globe. The text refers to the medieval debate on the location of the earthly paradise and suggests that the Garden of Eden still exists somewhere in the east, either on the equator or south of it.

The vignette (probably not from Fra Mauro's hand, perhaps by the Venetian artist Leonardo Bellini) is placed in the bottom left corner (consequently in one of the eastern corners of the map, which has south at the top). It shows paradise as a circular walled garden. Inside, God is seen commanding Adam and Eve, who are still naked and without a sense of shame, not to touch the Tree of the Knowledge of Good and Evil. The angel standing by the entrance hints at the Fall that is to come. The water from the single spring flows from the middle of the garden to separate into the four rivers immediately outside the walls (Fig 58). The rest of the earth, outside paradise, is represented by the mountainous landscape next to the circular garden and corresponds to the earth displayed in detail on the central map. It is not yet inhabited, since the vignette portrays the world before the Fall (Fig 61).

Both paradise and the rest of the earth, however, are surrounded by the same outer ocean and connected by the four rivers, the source of all life, which flow out from the Garden of Eden to water the whole world. In this way the vignette shows that the inaccessible paradise, which does not feature in the inhabited and known earth

Fig 58 (left) *Detail of Fig 59: the earthly paradise.*

that is represented in full cartographical detail in the main map, is both contiguous to, and separate from, the world of the geographers. With his vignette Fra Mauro suggested that paradise belonged to an inaccessible eastern *nowhere*, and not to somewhere in the known world. By depicting paradise on a quite different plane than the contemporary inhabited earth portrayed in

Fig 59 *World map by Fra Mauro, Venice, c.1450. Venice, Biblioteca Nazionale Marciana.*

the main map, he also displayed an acute awareness of the temporal chasm decisively separating the lost paradise of delights from the human realm of his time.

Bibliographic Essay

◆

Columbus's remarks on paradise are found in L. Cecil Jane, trans. and ed., *Select Documents Illustrating the Four Voyages of Columbus*, 2 vols (London: The Hakluyt Society, 1930–33), II (1933), pp.34–8.

The literature on Dante's geography and astronomy is vast: see, for example, Brenda D. Schildgen, *Dante and the Orient* (Urbana: University of Illinois Press, 2002), and Bruno Nardi, 'Il mito dell'Eden', in his *Saggi di filosofia dantesca*, 2nd edn (Florence: La Nuova Italia, 1967), pp.311–40.

There is an abundant literature on the thirteenth-century philosophical and scientific revolution. See, for example, the bibliography in Michael Haren, *Medieval Thought: The Western Intellectual Tradition from Antiquity to the Thirteenth Century*, 2nd edn (Toronto-Buffalo: University of Toronto Press, 1992). The assimilation of Aristotelianism, considered by many to be a potential threat to the Christian faith, was by no means an untroubled process, as can be seen from the series of ecclesiastical condemnations, culminating in the 219 doctrines condemned by the bishop of Paris in 1277. For the geographical side see John K. Wright, *The Geographical Lore of the Time of the Crusades: A Study in the History of Medieval Science and Tradition in Western Europe* (New York: American Geographical Society, 1925; repr. New York: Dover Publications, 1965), and Reuven S. Avi-Yonah, *The Aristotelian Revolution: A Study of the Transformation of Medieval Cosmology, 1150–1250* (PhD dissertation, Harvard University, 1986). The 'geographical renaissance' was not, however, a radical break with the earlier tradition, since the process of assimilation of Aristotelian cosmology lasted for several decades, and geographical studies still depended on the same classical sources and the writings of the Fathers of the early Christian Church which were already known.

For early writers praising the perfect climate in paradise see Howard Rollin Patch, *The Other World, According to Descriptions in Medieval Literature* (Cambridge, MA: Harvard University Press, 1950), pp.134–74. Isidore's dictum about it (*Etymologiae*, II, XIV.3.2–3) was repeated by a number of encyclopedists: Vincent of Beauvais, Ranulph Higden, Brunetto Latini and Bartholomeus Anglicus.

On zonal maps see the discussion in David Woodward, 'Medieval *Mappaemundi*', in J. B. Harley and David Woodward, eds., *The History of Cartography*, I: *Cartography in Prehistoric, Ancient and Medieval Europe and the Mediterranean* (Chicago University Press, 1987), pp.296–7, 353–5. Reproductions of several medieval zonal maps may be found, for example, in Patrick Gautier Dalché, '*Mappae mundi* antérieures au XIIIe siècle dans les manuscrits latins de la Bibliothèque Nationale de France', *Scriptorium*, 52:1 (1998), pp.102–61, plates 25–7, 30–2. On the Arnstein Bible maps see Evelyn Edson, *Mapping Time and Space* (London: British Library, 1997, 1999), pp.92–4. On the 'Brendan map' see Anna-Dorothee von den Brincken, 'Das Weltbild des irischen Seefahrer-Heiligen Brendan in der Sicht des 12. Jahrhunderts', *Cartographia Helvetica*, 21 (January 2000), pp.17–21.

The origin of the navigational charts is uncertain and much discussed. The genre is far less homogeneous than the impression given in the brief description here, and a number of changes took place in the course of the fourteenth and fifteenth centuries. See

Fig 60 (above) *Detail of Fig 59: the number of heavens.*

Tony Campbell, 'Portolan Charts from the Late Thirteenth Century to 1500', in Harley and Woodward, eds., *History of Cartography*, I (1987), pp.371–463; Patrick Gautier Dalché, *Carte marine et Portulan au XIIe siècle. Le «Liber de existencia riveriarum et forma maris nostris Mediterranei», (Pise, circa 1200)* (Rome: École française de Rome, 1995), suggests that the charts emerged a century earlier than is generally thought. For a list of Vesconte's maps see Woodward, 'Medieval *Mappaemundi*' (1987), pp.363–4. See also Evelyn Edson, 'Reviving the Crusade in the Fourteenth Century: Sanudo's Schemes and Vesconte's Maps', in Rosamund S. Allen, ed., *Eastward Bound. Medieval Travel and Travellers 1050–1500* (Manchester: Manchester University Press, 2004), pp.131–4.

On the so-called 'transitional period' in the history of cartography (1300–1460), see

Woodward, 'Medieval *Mappaemundi*' (1987), pp.314–18, and Evelyn Edson, *The World Map 1300–1492: The Persistence of Tradition and Transformation* (Baltimore: Johns Hopkins University Press, 2007).

On the Catalan Estense map see *Il mappamondo catalano estense / Die Katalanische Estense-Weltkarte*, Kommentar, Ernesto Milano; Transkription des Orginaltextes, Annalisa Battini (Dietikon-Zurich: Urs Graf, 1995).

On Fra Mauro's map see Piero Falchetta, *The Fra Mauro World Map* (Turnhout: Brepols, 2006) and Angelo Cattaneo, *Fra Mauro's Mappa Mundi and Fifteenth-Century Venice* (Turnhout: Brepols, 2011). On the attribution of the vignette to Leonardo Bellini, see Angelo Cattaneo, 'God in This World: the Earthly Paradise in Fra Mauro's Mappamundi Illuminated by Leonardo Bellini', *Imago Mundi*, 55 (2003), pp.121–6, Plates 9–11; and Susy Marcon, 'Il Mappamondo di Fra Mauro e Leonardo Bellini', in Mario Piantoni and Laura de Rossi, eds., *Per l'arte da Venezia all'Europa. Studi in onore di Giuseppe Maria Pilo* (Venice: Edizioni della Laguna, 2001), pp.103–8.

Fig 61 (below) *Detail of Fig 59: the earth outside the Garden of Eden.*

CHAPTER 6

PINNING DOWN PARADISE

Saint Brendan and his fellow monks set sail from their monastery. Once they left the harbour, they shipped their oars, tied the rudder and left the sails spread. They waited for God to pilot the boat. When they got a wind, they did not know from what direction it came or in which direction the boat was heading. They journeyed for seven years, making fantastic discoveries. They encountered extraordinary sights. They met beasts of immense size and mighty monsters. They disembarked on islands populated by bizarre creatures. They eventually reached a delightful land of bliss and eternal light. Their willingness to put their trust in God, instead of pursuing a specific route, allowed the divine hand to turn their prow towards the island of paradise.

FROM THE *NAVIGATIO SANCTI BRENDANI*,
COMPOSED BETWEEN THE EIGHTH
AND THE TENTH CENTURY

Armenia
Maior

Assyria

Mesopotamia

fia maior.

EVPHRATES · F ·

TIGRIS · F ·

A

Iudaea

ra=

Sur desert ·

GEHON ·

Chus
· n ·
Aethiopia

B

Heuilat

PHISON

Arabia

ptus

Mare
1

Mare
Persicum

FROM PARADISE PRESENT TO PARADISE PAST

The story of St Brendan was very popular in the Middle Ages. The ocean journeys of a group of adventurous monks searching for paradise articulated the ideals of monastic life and represented man's vocation to reach the kingdom of heaven. The legend contains various hints that Brendan's quest for Adam's Garden of Eden was in fact a search for the heavenly abode promised by God to his saints at the end of time. Christians knew very well that the earthly paradise of Adam and Eve was forever lost to humankind and that the only possible journey back to it was by following the flow of time that began in Eden and would end in heaven, through the Passion of Christ in Jerusalem.

In the mid-fifteenth century Fra Mauro depicted the inaccessible Garden of Eden as outside the inhabited world and distanced in the past, and on a quite different plane from the contemporary human realm portrayed in his main map (Fig 59). From around 1500, however, the idea that paradise existed in the past came to be interpreted by biblical commentators in a more explicit but narrower way. The hidden yet still existing paradise had until then been perceived both as a mark of divine goodness and as a reminder of the tragic consequences of sin. Over the course of the sixteenth century belief in a contemporary Garden of Eden declined, with the general tendency in exegesis being to admit that Eden was no longer part of the present world.

Medieval debate had left unresolved all sorts of problems relating to the geography of paradise, most notably the impossibility of identifying its exact site and of finding a credible view about its altitude. To deal with such unresolved conundrums, biblical commentators turned away from the geographical horizons of the present and looked instead for a geography of the past. The idea of a contemporary and inaccessible paradise shifted to the concept of a paradise distant in time, now lost but formerly in a region within reach. Explaining the problem of its location in this way provided the only means of preserving the integrity of a literal and historical reading of Genesis, and thus of leaving intact the authority of Scripture. The waning of belief in an extant earthly paradise represented a major shift in religious thought. It also accompanied the opening up of new geographical horizons, and paralleled important changes in mapping practice.

A RADICAL CHANGE IN EUROPEAN CARTOGRAPHY

In 1406 a Byzantine manuscript of Ptolemy's *Geography* arrived in Venice from Constantinople. By the next year, the Florentine Jacopo Angelo had turned the Greek text into Latin, making it available to a significantly wider readership in the West. Ptolemy, a second-century AD Alexandrian astronomer, included in his *Geography* detailed instructions for different ways of portraying the spherical earth on a flat surface according to mathematical and astronomical principles. The work also featured lists of coordinates of latitude and longitude for thousands of cities,

Previous page: *Map of the location of Eden inserted into* Antoine Regnault's Discours du Voyage d'outre mer au St. Sépulcre de Jérusalem et autres lieux de la Terre Saincte *(Lyons: [n. pub.], 1573). Detail of Fig 68: the Garden of Eden in the Middle East. London, British Library, G.2824.*

towns and major natural features, grouped into the three parts of the known world: Europe, Africa and Asia. Ptolemy's *Geography* is generally assumed to have been lost to Western Europe until the fifteenth century, but hints have been accumulating that suggest that some knowledge of the text may have survived in closed scholarly circles from late antiquity up to the twelfth century. For example, references to the *Geography* have survived in texts written in late fourth-century Rome (Ammianus Marcellinus), in Italy in the sixth century (Cassiodorus and Jordanes), in the Carolingian commentaries on Martianus Capella and the twelfth-century writings of Iohannes Tzetzes, as well as in the Byzantine Empire in both the sixth and again in the ninth centuries – not forgetting Latin translations from the Arabic of the work of scholars such as Al-Khwarizmi. Geographical coordinates had already been used for some time by astrologers in connection with their study of the influence of the heavens. Roger Bacon discussed the use of latitudes and longitudes in mapping procedure, and may even have constructed a map on the basis of some sort of grid. The system of coordinates, however, was not rigorously applied in cartography, as medieval mapmakers had been drawing their *mappae mundi* according to a qualitative conception of space and its subordination to historical time. Only when new horizons emerged in the fifteenth century did mathematics and maps come together once again.

Jacopo Angelo's Latin translation did not feature maps, but these (one world map and 26 regional maps) were soon being drawn to illustrate subsequent manuscripts. In 1477 the first printed edition with maps was published in Bologna. It was followed by another printed in Rome in 1478, and by the version with some modern maps compiled by Nicholaus Germanus and printed in Ulm by Lienhart Holle in 1482 and 1486 (Fig 62). The maps, drawn on geometrical projections, were totally unlike anything seen before in the medieval West.

The recovery of the *Geography* and its maps in the early fifteenth century by Western Europe was, in the longer term, of unparalleled significance, for the Ptolemaic model became the basis of modern cartography. By the beginning of the fifteenth century, some of the most fundamental characteristics of *mappae mundi* had already become diluted, as we saw with Fra Mauro's map. First to go was the eastern orientation. On the old *mappa mundi*, where the placing of east at the top of the map was linked to the space–time configuration of the world, the presence of paradise crowned the unfolding of world history from east to west. Ptolemy's instructions were for the construction of maps with north at the top, and the *Geography*'s growing influence effectively sanctioned the loss of that eastern privilege on world maps. Eventually, the change of orientation marked the definitive divorce between history and geography. Consequently the representation of historical time on maps shifted from its former all-embracing nature to an episodic significance.

Ptolemaic maps, that is, maps based on projections modelled on Ptolemy's or constructed in such a way as to give at least the illusion of a projection or a graphic perspective, came to express the temporal dimension in a markedly different way from medieval *mappae mundi*. On a Ptolemaic map geography was cleared from the

Fig 62 (overleaf) *World map on Ptolemy's second projection, from Claudius Ptolemaeus,* Cosmographia *(Ulm: Lienart Holle, 1486). London, British Library, 1C.9303.*

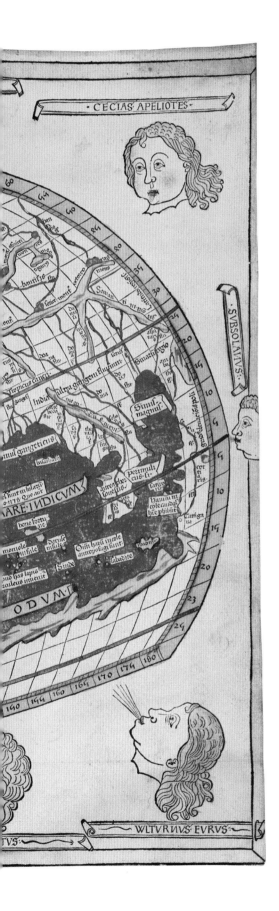

domination of historical time. The relationship between space and time remained intimate, but it was now mathematically defined. The astronomical measurement of time determined the parallels and meridians that structured the map and measured space itself.

Whereas a fully-fledged medieval *mappa mundi* depicted past events and places – including those mentioned in the Bible – the development of a methodical system of astronomical coordinates favoured the inclusion on maps of contemporary features only. At the same time, maps from the second half of the fifteenth century onwards had to take into account the increased rate at which geographical information about the world was reaching the West through the search for new commercial routes and other voyages (a process which culminated in the discovery of the New World). Maps were no longer required to present a stable image of a world into which the history of salvation could be incorporated, as in the medieval tradition. Knowledge, moreover, had become so much greater that it was difficult to display in a single visual narrative.

Maps had become provisional documents, showing, for a specific moment in time, a world that needed to be constantly redrawn in the light of further discoveries. Any transhistorical quality was lost. Instead of a comprehensive space–time image, in which geography was combined with historical time, maps of the world from the late fifteenth century onwards mirrored the surface of an earth measured in units of astronomical time alone.

On medieval *mappae mundi*, history had accorded privilege to individual places depending on the events that had occurred there. Core and periphery were distinguished. The central place was not necessarily geometrically centred, but was made identifiable through the size and the nature of the map sign. Some towns, such as those in the vicinity of the map's origin, and Jerusalem, were displayed as more important than others. On a Ptolemaic map, in contrast, space defined by mathematical astronomy was homogeneous and indifferent to human history. No one point on the map was any more important than any other.

On a map of the world ruled by computable coordinates defined by astronomical time, whose function was to give accurately measured and correctly proportioned distances between places, there was no room for an inaccessible and unlocatable earthly paradise. The compilers of the *mappae mundi* had accepted the paradox of mapping the Garden of Eden because of its importance as the scene of the Fall, simply suggesting its contiguity to the inhabited earth. Renaissance mapmakers found it difficult to include that primordial feature on a modern map that mirrored the surface of the contemporary world, displayed on an east–west span of 12 hours (the interval between the two extreme meridians) and a north–south span based on the variation in length of day and the climatic zones – criteria which in both cases were natural and not historical. Most definitively the earthly paradise, which had been shown on medieval maps as beyond the boundaries of the inhabited and known part of the earth, could not be included on a map that by definition featured only such a part, the *oecumene*.

CHANGING THEOLOGY

While the disappearance of the earthly paradise from world maps at the end of the fifteenth century was part of a changing cartographical context, it was also a function of changes in theological thinking. Above all, it reflected the slow decline of the idea that the Garden of Eden still survived somewhere on earth.

Renaissance explorers were disclosing new lands where there was no trace of the biblical paradise – neither in India, Ethiopia, China, Japan, nor the New World. None of them really intended, or thought they could, discover the location of Eden and recapture for humankind the lost paradise of delight. In the previous chapter, we have seen that Christopher Columbus might well have wondered in his journal if he were close to the Garden of Eden, but would not have seriously thought of it as a place to travel to. The earthly paradise was known to be inaccessible and beyond the horizon for ordinary humans, not to be found by anyone around the corner, and this fact was confirmed by geographical discoveries. However, it was not the failure of its discovery alone that eventually expunged the presence of Eden from the cartographers' maps of the world. The intellectual search for the site of the Garden of Eden had already presented biblical exegetes with huge difficulties well before fifteenth- and sixteenth-century merchants and travellers started to bring news of their experiences back to Europe. The problem for the theologians, as we have seen, was the wide range of contradictions and paradoxes that were contained in the very idea of an earthly Eden.

An attempt to provide a rational interpretation of Genesis that matched the geographical lore of the age was made by some sixteenth-century scholars, including Vadianus (Joachim Van Watt), the Swiss humanist and a follower of Zwingli; Goropius Becanus (Jan van Gorp), the Flemish philosopher, physician, antiquarian and linguist; Ludovicus Fidelis, a Flemish professor of theology; Ludovico Nogarola, a humanist and scholar from Verona who attended the Council of Trent; and Juan de Pineda, a Spanish Jesuit and a biblical exegete and historian. They all argued that paradise on earth referred to the blessed state experienced by Adam and Eve before their sin, and that Eden, instead of being a specific location, had once encompassed the entire earth before God cursed it. Whereas in the Middle Ages it was thought that the divine curse had spared a still existing Eden, it was now suggested that the curse had ruined paradise itself, meaning the whole earth. Mapping means to outline, to contour, to frame; and had the whole-earth paradise theory prevailed, a paradise comprising the entire earthly space, with no boundaries that could outline it, would have become unmappable.

The idea that the Garden of Eden did not comprise a limited and particular area and that the beauty, plenty and delights associated with it in Scripture had been common to the whole earth prior to the Fall solved many difficulties. Not least among these was the problem of a localised Garden of Eden left empty and unused after Adam's sin. That doctrine, however, albeit rationally appealing, went against the letter of Scripture, in particular against the explicit reference in Genesis to the expulsion of Adam and Eve from paradise. This now had to be interpreted allegorically, as a reference to a change in the human condition.

In the 1530s the Protestant reformer Martin Luther shared with those who believed in a whole-earth paradise the idea that sin had brought about the ruin of nature. At the same time Luther was a passionate defender of the historical meaning of Scripture, and he found it hard to reject the letter of the biblical text. When he read in Genesis that Adam was driven out of a particular place, and that an angel had been put on guard at the entrance to paradise, he was prompted to suggest that paradise had once occupied a specific land. For him the biblical account of the expulsion implied the existence of some sort of boundary between paradise and the rest of the earth.

After the Fall, Luther suggested, the Garden of Eden had remained inaccessible to humankind, guarded by the Cherubim and the flaming sword. Eventually, at the time of the Flood, even the remains of paradise were completely destroyed. As the Garden of Eden was wiped out by the Flood, it was pointless, in Luther's view, to speculate about its exact location. The problem of the identification of the four rivers of paradise, for example, was solved by the argument that the rivers were affected by the Flood's destruction.

In the first complete edition of Luther's translation of the Bible, published in Wittenberg in 1534, we see a woodcut of the Garden of Eden, which corresponds to Luther's reading of the biblical text (Fig 63). The illustration is a portrait of the perfect and uncorrupted universe at end of the week of creation. Adam and Eve stand naked in a pleasant landscape, rich in flora and fauna (Fig 64). They are themselves pure, perfect and innocent like the world in which they dwell in peaceful harmony. All kinds of obedient animals surround them, including the snake, then standing upright rather than crawling along the ground as it was condemned to do after the Fall. The garden is represented as a huge region, part of a paradise-like earth with clearly depicted coastal outlines, islands and mountains, while God the Father, radiating light and clothed in a royal mantle, with long hair and flowing beard, blesses the universe below him.

After the Fall God cursed Eden and the earth, whereupon, according to Luther, Eden lost its fertility and mankind lost its Eden. The image printed in various editions

of Luther's Bible appears to be more of a pictorial and fictional representation of a lost world than a map showing exactly where Eden lay. It would be vain to attempt to recognise any familiar geographical features. But this was Luther's point: the face of the earth had dramatically changed since the Flood and Eden had been irrevocably destroyed. This is the tragedy brought about by human sin. Paradise was cursed; paradise was flooded; paradise was no more.

Luther's belief that paradise had disappeared and that the surface of the earth had radically changed as a consequence of sin was consistent with his more general theological views. In his view God's entire creation had been corrupted by the sin that brought about the Fall (and later the Flood) and was now awaiting final restoration. A divine curse was inflicted on both nature and humankind: the garden of delight vanished, the four rivers of paradise became tainted and the earth lost its fertility, in the same way as man had lost all his innocence and immortality and his body became wretchedly corrupted. After the Fall, the Garden of Eden brought forth thorns and thistles, and at the time of the Flood even its remains were destroyed. The pristine beauty of the world was ruined as a consequence of human wickedness. It would be impossible for a Lutheran to expect to find paradise on maps referring to the earth after the Fall. Nevertheless, Luther's insistence on both keeping to the letter of the Bible and describing Eden as a vast and yet specific region no longer in existence served to prepare the ground for a new cartography of paradise. A new approach to the problem of pinpointing Eden on a map was emerging.

And so paradise disappeared from world maps. Yet, from the sixteenth century onwards, new maps of paradise began to proliferate in European printed Bibles and historical atlases. How was this possible? It was the complex theological thinking of John Calvin that allowed paradise to be mapped in a different form from anything seen before.

Calvin believed, as did Luther, that the beauty and perfection of the earthly paradise had vanished because of sin. The world after the Fall was for him a chaotic and uncertain place, governed by the depravity of man and the hostility of nature. Calvin, however, tried to relieve his consternation about the tumultuous abyss into which humankind was thrown after the Fall. He insisted that, despite human sin, God cared about his creation and the world. This is why, to prevent humankind from being completely overwhelmed by despair, the Creator had scattered signs of his goodness over the earth. Such signs of order amidst chaos were to reassure man and to teach him about divine grace. One of these comforting traces of divine care for humankind was, in Calvin's view, what was left of the earthly paradise, and it was this remnant that could be shown on a map. Calvin pointed to that sign of divine benevolence, mapping the rivers of paradise still flowing in Mesopotamia, a fertile and beautiful place, praised by classical authors. Something, even after the Flood, had remained of the original geography of Eden; in the same way that human nature, however deformed and damaged as a result of sin, preserved some aspects of God's image.

Calvin's map of the rivers of paradise illustrated his *Commentary on Genesis* printed in Geneva in 1553 and 1554 (Fig 65). The map was an integral part of his theological discourse, since it was introduced in the text as a reassurance to humankind of God's benevolence and of the importance of earthly life. By the continuing presence of the rivers of paradise, God made it clear that he still provided humankind with a home on earth for the duration of its pilgrimage to heaven.

With Calvin's new interpretation, all the details of the biblical narrative seemed to fall into place. Genesis specifies that the earthly paradise was in the east because Moses (the traditional author of the first five books of the Bible, which include Genesis) was near the Holy Land when he was writing the Pentateuch, and the Mesopotamian Eden was to the east of it. The text says that 'a river went out of Eden to water the garden'. That river, according to Calvin, flowed through paradise as a single stream, dividing outside paradise – both upstream and downstream – into two branches, making four rivers in all. To support this interpretation, Calvin went back to the term used in the Vulgate to indicate the four rivers, namely 'heads' (*capita*, in Latin). Heads of the rivers, for Calvin, meant the two channels that brought the water to paradise *and* the two channels which discharged it into the sea. The four 'heads' of the text (*quattuor capita*) branched from the single river within paradise, with the two upper streams flowing from their sources into the confluence and the two lower ones flowing from it towards the Persian Gulf. On the map two separate rivers, the Tigris

Fig 65 *John Calvin's map of the location of Eden from his* Commentaire ... sur le premier livre de Moyse, dit Genèse *(Geneva: Ian Gerard, 1553, 2nd edn 1554), p.33. London, British Library, 1016.1.3.*

naissent, que les issues, par lesquelles ils se deschargent en la mer. Ia autresfois a
esté Euphrates conioint auec le Tygre qui tôboit dedans luy: tellemêt qu'on pou
uoit dire à bon droit que c'estoit vn fleuue separé en quatre chefs. Principalement
si on m'accorde ce qui est manifeste à tous, que Moyse n'a point parlé subtilemêt
ny à la façon des Philosophes, mais populairemêt, afin que le plus rude qui y fust
le peust entêdre. En ceste façon il a appellé au premier chapitre le soleil & la lune
Les deux grans luminaires: non pas que la lune surmonte les autres Planettes en
grandeur, mais pource que cômunement par le regard on l'estime plus grande.
Ie mettray icy vne figure deuant les yeux, par laquelle on pourra entendre où i'e-
stime que Moyse met Paradis.

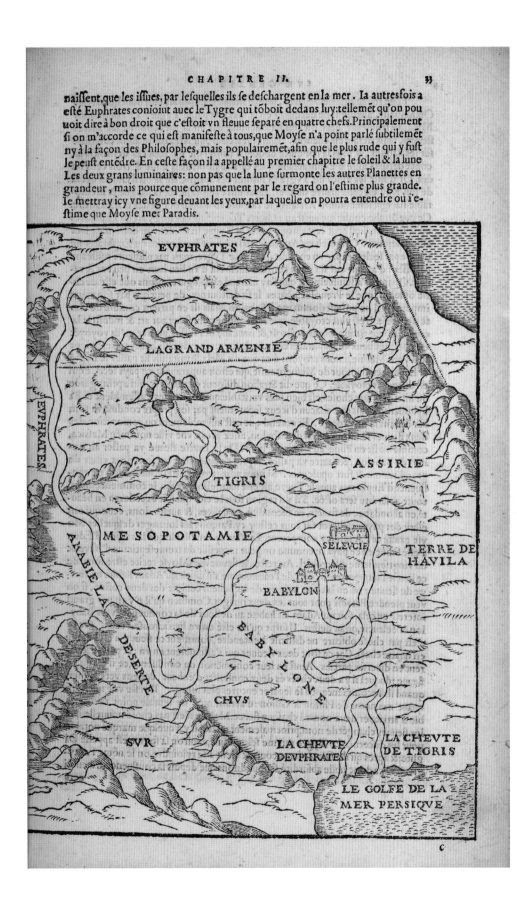

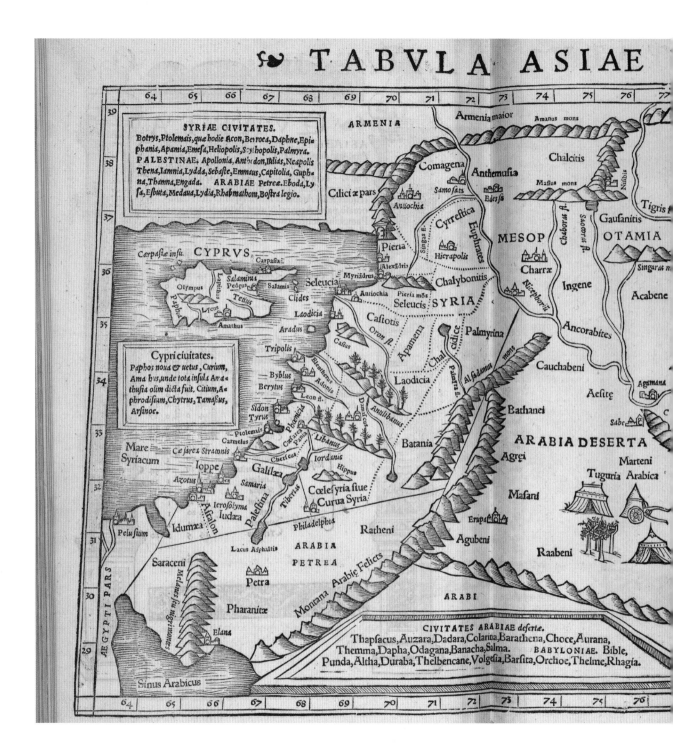

and the Euphrates, join into a single stream that flows through paradise (unmarked on the map). This then divides again into two branches, the Gihon and the Pison, which flow into the Persian Gulf, making four rivers in all.

Calvin's map shows the confluence of the Tigris and the Euphrates north of Seleucia, their separation to create an island and their joining again south of the city

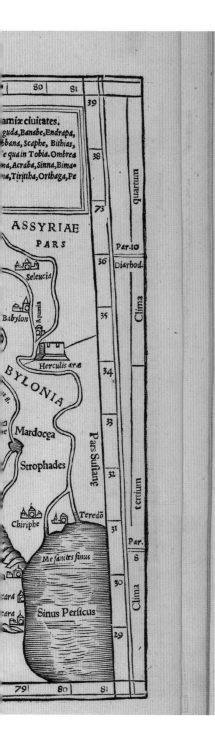

of Babylon. Downstream the two rivers again divided to reach the Persian Gulf in two outfalls, marked on the map as *la cheute d'Euphrates* and *la cheute de Tigris*. The lands of Havilah and Cush, which had been placed in far eastern Asia and equatorial Africa by earlier Christian scholars, were situated by Calvin in Mesopotamia. The huge bend made by the Tigris south of Babylon effectively encompasses the land of Havilah in the same way as the Pison was said to do in the Genesis text. Calvin avoided pinpointing the exact site of paradise, saying that the precise location of Adam's dwelling did not really matter. For him, it was sufficient to show the general area of the remnant of Eden and how the single river divided into four branches.

Calvin's exegetical source was probably Augustinus Steuchus, known as Eugubinus. An influential Roman churchman and head of the Vatican Library, he was the first exegete to claim explicitly, in his commentary on the Pentateuch (a work of humanist biblical exegesis titled *Recognitio Veteris Testamenti ad hebraicam veritatem* and printed in Venice in 1529), that the earthly paradise had actually disappeared and that the single stream of paradise branched into four courses – in the sense that two rivers first came together and then separated (a reversal of the medieval concept of a single source from which four rivers flowed out in four directions). Calvin's cartographical source was surely Ptolemy. The Fourth Map of Asia, from printed editions of Ptolemy's *Geography*, showed the eastern Mediterranean and the Middle East from Cyprus to Babylon (Fig 66). It provided Calvin with the two key points of his Edenic geography: the four river heads and the great bend of the River Pison. Calvin made one crucial change, however. In order to create the single stream mentioned in Genesis he made a link between the Tigris and the Euphrates, well above their confluence, to imply that paradise occupied the island thus formed in that short stretch of the single river. From his map paradise is made to appear to be located in Mesopotamia, by definition 'the land between two rivers', and at the same time to be watered by a single stream (Fig 65).

Calvin's geography of paradise followed from his conviction that God's light still shone in the midst of darkness. Despite the fact that paradise was not explicitly indicated, Calvin's map proved to be the first in a long series of regional maps dealing with the location of Eden. Paradise was both lost from the face of the earth and found in Mesopotamia. Its archaeological remains could now be located in a precise way.

Fig 66 *Sebastian Münster's version of Ptolemy's* Tabula Quarta Asiae *from Claudius Ptolemaeus,* Geographia universalis, *eds Sebastian Münster and Bilibaldus Pirckheimer (Basle: Henricus Petrus, 1540). London, British Library, Maps C.1.c.2.(1).*

Visual Interlude
Paradise in Mesopotamia

◆

Calvin's theological thought and his rhetorical use of Renaissance mapping relaunched the cartography of paradise, locating it in Mesopotamia. The map that he produced for his *Commentary on Genesis* in 1553–4, however, reflected only the traces that betrayed the former existence of the lost Garden of Eden, rather than its exact site. Adam was placed, Calvin explained, either on the island formed by the confluence of the Tigris and the Euphrates or in the area immediately north of the branch that connected the two rivers. The main purpose of his map was not so much to pinpoint paradise, but to show that its rivers had remained unchanged despite the curse on the earth and the destruction brought about by the Fall and the Flood. His map identified the general region in which Eden had once existed to show that this region was geographically real and that the area continued to exist. In his effort to trace the courses of the four rivers, however, Calvin found himself giving an implicit indication of where the garden was most likely to have been situated. Later exegetes and mapmakers would propose various other locations and compile new maps of paradise, trying to make explicit what Calvin had deliberately left unsaid.

In the years after Calvin, as maps began to carry a vignette or a place name specifying the precise site of the former garden, they took on a more overtly historical character, providing the basis for one of the commonest map subjects in the second half of the sixteenth century and throughout the seventeenth century. The paradise now made clearly visible on maps copied or derived from Calvin's was obviously a paradise past. In Geneva in 1560, Calvin's map of Eden had been redrawn and added to the complement of maps included in editions of the Geneva Bible, in order to help the reader visualise the place where human history had begun. The most important change was the addition of a tiny vignette of the Fall, for example on the map used in 1565 and 1566 by the Lyon publisher Sebastien Honoré in a French edition of the Geneva Bible (Fig 67). The explicitness of Honoré's image of Adam and Eve with the serpent and the Tree of Knowledge provided a direct link back to the biblical account, as well as an apparently exact indication of the site of the Garden of Eden. The creator of Honoré's map diverged from Calvin in another respect. He did not place the vignette of the Garden of Eden at the confluence of the Tigris and the Euphrates near Babylon and Seleucia, which Calvin had said was the most likely place for paradise. Instead it was set much further south, just below the name *Terre de Havilah* (Havilah was the most obvious reference on

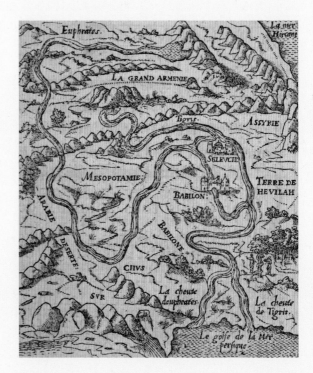

Calvin's map to Edenic geography) and to the east of the single river.

The tendency was to simplify Calvin's map for the sake of clarity. Another way in which this was done is illustrated by the map inserted in Antoine Regnault's account of his journey to the Holy Land, published in 1573 (Fig 68). On Regnault's map, which shows the whole Middle Eastern region and incorporates the Holy Land and the shores of the Mediterranean, as well as the Caspian and Black Seas, the geography of paradise has been reduced to a striking simplicity. Two rivers, the Tigris and the Euphrates, first join together to form the single river that flows through the large rectangular enclosure containing the garden of paradise, then divide again into the Gihon and the Pison (so labelled on the map). *A* marks the confluence, just outside paradise, of the Euphrates and Tigris rivers, and *B* the division of the single river into two branches, again just outside the Garden of Eden. Regnault shows Adam and Eve both within the garden, picking the forbidden fruit, and also outside it, being expelled. The lands surrounded by the streams of paradise, Havilah, Cush and Assyria, are also marked. On Regnault's map, as on other derivatives, Calvin's geography has been further simplified by the removal of the link north of Seleucia between the Tigris and the Euphrates. That link, which formed an island between Babylon and Seleucia, was the vital element in Calvin's argument that a single river of paradise flowed through Mesopotamia, a cartographical sleight of hand that would long continue to haunt the maps of Calvin's imitators. In actual fact, the most controversial aspect of the new model for the cartography of the earthly

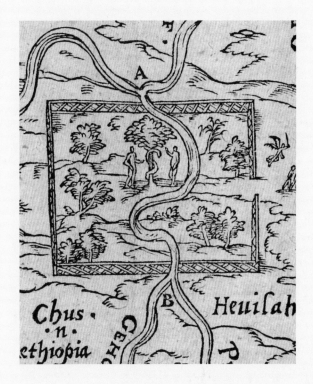

paradise established by Calvin's map proved to be the identification of the single river of paradise out of which the four rivers were said to branch. More generally, whereas Calvin had managed to combine advanced cartography with advanced exegesis, those who created maps showing the location of the Garden of Eden in the wake of Calvin's exegesis did so with little of his theological sophistication.

Fig 67 (opposite) *Variant of Calvin's map of the location of Eden from* La Saincte Bible *(Lyon: Sebastien Honoré, 1566), p.2r. London, British Library, C.23.e.10.*

Fig 68 (above and overleaf) *Map of the location of Eden inserted into Antoine Regnault's* Discours du Voyage d'outre mer au St. Sépulcre de Jérusalem et autres lieux de la Terre Saincte *(Lyon: [n. pub.], 1573). London, British Library, G.2824.*

Figure
métioée
en la pag.
150. qui
est de la
terre sain
cte.

Detant de regions que le ciel contient en son circuit, ceste cy est de si grande louäge exaucée par tous les Corographes, que de leur commune opinion, toutes les autres en bonté de terre, fertilité de bledz, toutes sortes de delices, & diuerses graces de nature elle est estimée de beaucoup auancer. A bon droit donques les louanges, desquelles Moyse si grandement honnore le Paradis, a ceste region principallement & sur toutes autres competer, & appartenir est manifeste : (en laquelle est vray semblable le lieu de Eden aucir esté si-tué, comme des c. 7. d'Esaie, & 17. d'Ezechiel se peut facilement colliger Neantmoins quant Moyse dict ce fleuue, sortir de ce lieu, i'esti-me qu'il se doit entendre du cours de l'eau: ne plus ne moins que s'il disoit Adam auoir habité la riue du fleuue ou la terre deça & delà par luy arrousée, si vous entendez le Paradis en l'vne & l'autre riue auoir esté situé. Et combien qu'il ne chaut pas beaucoup si Adá a habité le lieu d'en haut (auquel les deux fleuues tombent ensemble vers Babilô & Seleucie) ou celluy d embas, toutesfois nous suffira, icelluy auoir esté en ce lieu lequel estoit arrosé desdictes eaues, D'auantage il n'est pas beaucoup obscur, ny difficile a congnoi-stre comme ce fleuue ait esté diuisé en deux testes, ou bras. Car ce sont deux fleuues lesquelz premierement tombent en vn mesme lieu, puis sont conduitz en diuerses parties. A ceste raison en leur conionction, confluent, ou source, n'est qu'vn mesme fleuue : lequel a deux chefz, a sçauoir aux deux cours superieurs: puis encor deux autres vers la mer, quand derechef plus loing ilz sont separez. Mais vn doute nous reste encores, des noms de Phison, & Gehon, parce que lon a trouué n'estre raisonnable a chacun fleuue deux noms estre donnez. Toutesfois telle chose n'est ne inaccoustumée, ne certainement nouuelle, d'autant qu'il aduient souuent que les nôs des fleuues sont changez, principallement quand il y a quelque remarque notable, par laquelle l vn de l'autre peut facilemêt estre discer-né. Car le Tygris mesmement suyuãt la sentêce de Pline, alendroit de sa source & fontaine où il a son cours plus lentement, est appellé Diglito: puis apres ses diuers cours, quand les eaues sont retournées, & ensemblement sont meslées, est appellé Pasitigrin. Ne sera point donc absurde dire que le fleuue Tigris, du lieu auquel il est côioint auec l'autre a pris diuers nôs: principallemêt quand l'on s'apperçoit qu'il y a si grâde affinité dudit Pasitigre auec Phison, tellement qu'il est vray semblable le nom de Pasitigre estre quelque remarque de Indigenæ illius regionis illam appellant Phasim. C'est a dire les habitans d'icelle region l'appellent Phasis. Ce qui n'appartient pas mal a tou-tes les autres circonstances par lesquelles Moyse descript trois de ces fleuues. Phison enuironne toute la terre Heuilah, ou croit l'or. A bon droit dit que le fleuue Tigris la circuit pour les diuers & plusieurs destournemens dessous Mesopotamie. Et la terre Heuilah a mô jugement icy est prise, pour celle region laquelle est voisine a la Perse. Parce qu'au c.15. Moyse raconte que les Ismahelites ont pris leur siege, de Heuilah, iusques a Sur, laquelle attouche l'Egypte, de la partie par laquelle l'on va en Assyrie. Dont a bon droit se peut inferer, qu'Heuilah a la Susiane & Perse ait de appartenir. Car il est de necessité qu'icelle soit interieure a la Syrie, du costé qu'elle re-garde la mer Persique, & estre beaucoup distante de l'Egypte: veu que Moyse fait mention, de plusieurs peuples, lesquelz ont mis leurs sieges entre ses limites la. D'auãtage il est notoire a tous les Nabathiens, desquelz la est faicte mêtion estre aux limites des Perses. Don-ques maintenant a propos ce rapporte ce que Moyse afferme que l'or & les pierres pretieuses y croissent. Reste de dire quelque cho-se du Gehon, lequel Moyse dit, decourir par la terre de Chus, laquelle tous les interpretes tournent Ethiopie. Outreplus audict Moy-se la region des Madianites, auec celle part d'Arabie, laquelle luy côsine, sont comprises soubz ce mot Chus. De ce vient que sa femme de race Madianite, en vn autre endroit est appellée Ethiopisse: veu donc que le cours inferieur d'Euphrates, tô be vers ceste partie, ie ne voy point repugner a la verité & foy historique qu'elle ne soit comprise soubz ce nom Gehon. Tellement que le pur & simple sens de Moyse sera telle: Iardin d'Eden, duquel Adam fut possesseur, estre arrouse d'eaues, en tant que ce fleuue estoit en luy, & en cest en-droit estoit conduit en quatre chefz au rameaux.

Bibliographic Essay

─────────── ◆ ───────────

A good reference work on geographical ideas in the Renaissance is Jean-Marc Besse, *Les Grandeurs de la Terre: Aspects du savoir géographique à la Renaissance* (Lyons: ENS, 2003). More generally the reader may refer to Denis Cosgrove, *Apollo's Eye: A Cartographic Genealogy of the Earth in the Western Imagination* (Baltimore–London: The Johns Hopkins University Press, 2001). For a useful compendium of world maps see Rodney W. Shirley, *The Mapping of the World: Early Printed World Maps, 1472–1700* (London: Early World Press, 2001).

Ptolemy, in the *Geography*, describes in detail how to construct three different projections to enable the spherical (that is, three dimensional) globe to be represented to scale on a flat (that is, two dimensional) surface. On Ptolemy's *Geography* see Oswald A. W. Dilke, 'The culmination of Greek cartography in Ptolemy', in J. B. Harley and David Woodward, eds., *The History of Cartography*, I: *Cartography in Prehistoric, Ancient and Medieval Europe and the Mediterranean* (Chicago: University of Chicago Press, 1987), pp.177–200. For a critical introduction to the three books giving instructions for the construction of maps on a projection, and an English translation, see J. Lennart Berggren and Alexander Jones, *Ptolemy's* Geography: *An Annotated Translation of the Theoretical Chapters* (Princeton–Oxford: Princeton University Press, 2000). In recent years, Patrick Gautier Dalché has made a particular study of the transmission of Ptolemy from antiquity to the Renaissance. See, for example, his *La Géographie de Ptolémée en Occident (IVe–XVIe siècle)* (Turnhout: Brepols, 2009), and 'The Reception of Ptolemy's Geography (End of the Fourteenth to Beginning of the Sixteenth Century)', in David Woodward, ed., *The History of Cartography*, III: *Cartography in the Renaissance*, (University of Chicago Press, 2007), pp.285–364. On Roger Bacon and the use of a coordinate system, see David Woodward, with Herbert M. Howe, 'Roger Bacon on Geography and Cartography', in Jeremiah Hackett, ed., *Roger Bacon and the Sciences: Commemorative Essays* (Leiden: Brill, 1997), pp.199–222; Woodward, 'Roger Bacon's Terrestrial Coordinate System', *Annals of the Association of American Geographers*, 80 (1990), pp.109–122. On Jacopo Angelo's translation of Ptolemy's geographical work see, for example, Sebastiano Gentile, 'Umanesimo e cartografia: Tolomeo nel secolo XV', in Angelo Cattaneo, Diego Ramado Curto and André Ferrand Almeida, eds., *La cartografia europea tra primo Rinascimento e fine dell'Illuminismo* (Florence: Olschki, 2003), pp.3–18. On Ptolemy's printed editions see Tony Campbell, *The Earliest Printed Maps 1472–1500* (London: The British Library; Berkeley, CA: University of California Press, 1987), pp.122–38.

For the Renaissance promoters of the idea of a whole-paradise earth see Joseph Duncan, 'Paradise as the Whole Earth', *Journal of the History of Ideas*, 30 (1969), pp.171–86; and Joseph Duncan, *Milton's Earthly Paradise* (Minneapolis: University of Minnesota Press, 1972), pp.199–202. Authors discussed in this chapters include Augustinus Steuchus, *Recognitio Veteris Testamenti ad hebraicam veritatem* (Venice: Aldus, 1529); Martin Luther, *Lectures on Genesis Chapters 1–5*, in Jaroslav Pelikan, ed., *Luther's Works* (St Louis, MO: Concordia, 1958); *Genesisvorlesung*, Gustav Koffmane and Otto Reichert, eds., in *D. Martin Luthers Werke*, XLII (Weimar: Hermann Böhlaus Nachfolger, 1911) [Luther lectured on the first chapters of Genesis between 1535 and 1536]; John Calvin, *Commentaire [...] sur le premier livre de Moyse, dit Genese* (Geneva: Iean Gerard, 1554). The first English translation, *A Commentarie [...] upon the first booke of Moses called Genesis*, was produced by Thomas Tymme (London: John Harison and George Bishop, 1578). My understanding of Calvin here largely follows the interpretation of William J. Bouwsma in his *John Calvin: A Sixteenth-Century Portrait* (New York–Oxford: Oxford University Press, 1988). Of special interest are Elizabeth M. Ingram, 'Maps as Readers' Aids: Maps and Plans in Geneva Bibles', *Imago Mundi*, 45 (1993), pp.34–5, and Max Engammare, 'Portrait de l'exégète en géographe. La carte du paradis comme instrument herméneutique chez Calvin et ses contemporains', *Annali di storia dell'esegesi*, 13/2 (1996), pp.565–81.

CHAPTER 7

EVERYTHING CHANGES, NOTHING CHANGES

Macarius was born in imperial Rome into a wealthy and renowned patrician family. The day came for him to get married. His father had arranged everything, but Macarius had no intention of starting a family. On the day of his wedding, he fled the house. His father searched everywhere for him without any success. The boy remained hidden in the house of a family friend for a week before leaving the region. On his way Macarius met a venerable, white-haired gentleman, who turned out to be the angel Raphael. God was watching over his journey. After many adventures he was led to a cave, not far from the Garden of Eden, where he found two lion cubs, with their mother lying dead beside them. Macarius dragged her outside the cave and buried her. He then cared for the little lions as if they were his own sons.

FROM THE *VITA FABULOSA SANCTI MACARII ROMANI*,
DATE UNCERTAIN

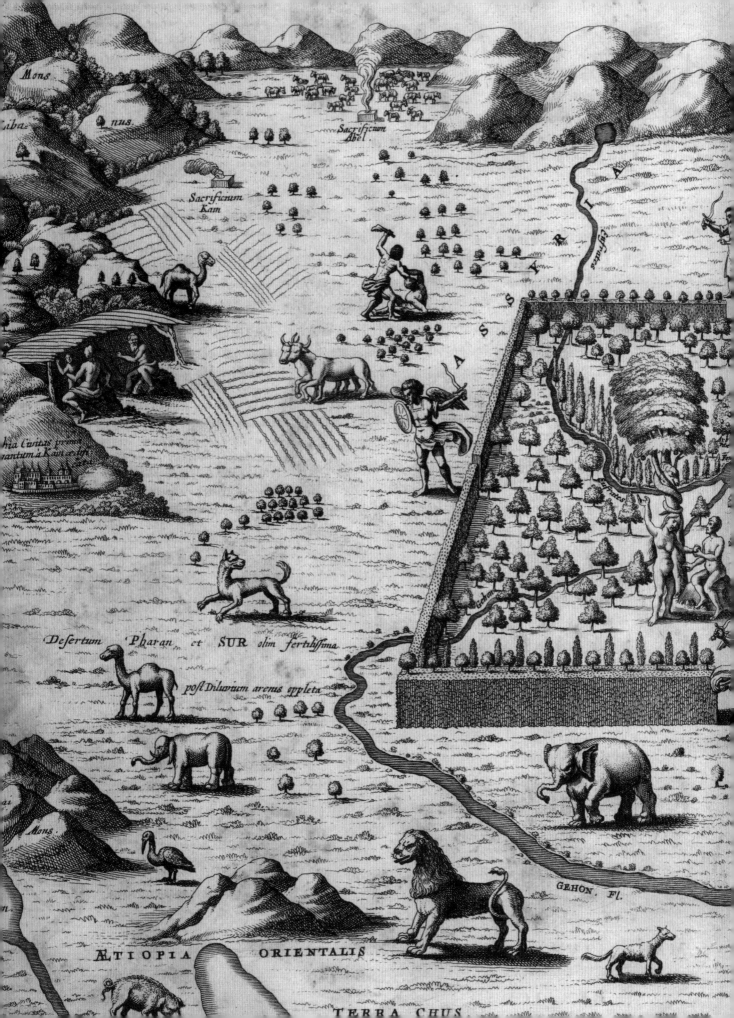

Mons

nus.

Sacrificium
Abel

Sacrificium
Kam

hia Civitas prima
antium à Kam est

Desertum Pharan et SUR olim fertilissima

post Diluvium arenis oppleta

Mons

GEHON. FL.

ÆTIOPIA ORIENTALIS

TERRA CHUS

SACRED GEOGRAPHY

According to the legend, the holy hermit Macarius did not want to start a family in Rome; but eventually he found himself entrusted with the care of two lion cubs, and thus with a young family, however unusual, and in an unforeseen setting – a cave near paradise on earth. Macarius chose a different path, but still ended up at the same place: he had no intention of starting a family, but eventually he acquired a 'kind of' family after all. The change already noted from the *mappae mundi*, with their depiction of a whole earth that included Eden, to the regional maps of the sixteenth century and later, led to the same outcome but by a different route: a new cartography of paradise.

This change reflected primarily a theological shift. The medieval idea that the Garden of Eden belonged to the present world had been largely abandoned. Preoccupation with the original site of a lost paradise was left to 'biblical archaeologists', who attempted to excavate that site from a few lines of text in Genesis. The rupture between the medieval and the modern mapping of paradise was soon complete. Yet there is a quality about the changing image of the Garden of Eden in European maps since the sixteenth century that reminds one of a sentence in Giuseppe Tomasi di Lampedusa's novel, *Il Gattopardo* (*The Leopard*): 'If we want things to stay as they are, things will have to change'. The novel chronicles changes in nineteenth-century Sicilian life and society during the Italian *Risorgimento*, when the nobility had to accept the new reality of the Kingdom of Italy in order to make things both change and stay the same. Likewise the adoption of Ptolemy's cartographical techniques in the Renaissance, which encouraged mapmakers to let astronomical measurement of time and not the narrative of historical progression govern the representation of space, was soon made to accommodate Christian belief. Maps showing the earthly paradise's location were compiled in the context of both sacred geography (to illustrate the Bible and biblical commentary) and historical geography (as maps in historical atlases).

From the sixteenth century onwards, interest in sacred geography – the use of contemporary geographical knowledge to identify and describe lands and countries mentioned in the Bible – was reinforced by a renewed concern, especially in Protestant circles, to explain the literal sense of the Bible. Biblical historical geography now constituted a specialised branch of historical knowledge, structured by combining biblical and secular learning. Moreover, the renewed emphasis on the literal and historical interpretation of the Bible matched the widespread humanist concern for textual clarity. Explanatory historical maps were drawn and printed to accompany editions of the Bible and biblical commentaries. The commercialisation of these Bibles was a significant aspect of the Renaissance culture of print, and of the Protestant effort to spread the knowledge of Scripture.

The new cartographical genre of the historical atlas emerged in the final quarter of the sixteenth century as a platform on which the past, classical as well as biblical, could be displayed. The historical atlas was a collection of maps that focused on particular themes or eras in history. Different ages or different historical themes were represented independently, map by map – quite unlike the all-embracing medieval

Previous page: *Athanasius Kircher's map* Topographia paradisi terrestris iuxta mentem et coniecturas authoris, *from his* Arca Noë *(Amsterdam: Ianssonius, 1675), between pp.196–7. London, British Library, 460.c.9. Detail of Fig 78: the Fall; Adam and Eve living as farmers away from the Garden of Eden; the sacrifice of Abel; his murder by Cain; the city of Enoch; various animals.*

mappae mundi, on which past and present were layered on to a single geographical landscape. In the historical atlas topics such as the peregrinations of the Patriarchs, the voyages of St Paul, the martial exploits of Aeneas and of Alexander the Great and the emergence of original sin in the Garden of Eden were presented as a series of selected vignettes, rather than being interwoven and intermixed with scenes and places important for other reasons.

By 1579, when Abraham Ortelius started work on the *Parergon* – a series of maps and views of the ancient world meant to accompany his *Theatrum orbis terrarum* (Theatre of the World), but which soon turned into an independent work – where he described geography as 'the eye of history', the transition from the separate historical map to the historical atlas was complete. Everything had to change so that nothing would change. New cartographical techniques were introduced, but there was no slackening in the zeal with which the authority of Scripture was defended in maps.

VARIATIONS ON THE MESOPOTAMIAN THEME

Biblical scholars took seriously the question of where Eden had once been, and invested much philological and exegetical learning in their attempt to make biblical text and geographical and cartographical science agree. To find the correct location for paradise was essential if the historical truth of the biblical account was to be upheld. Faith itself was at stake.

For a couple of centuries after Calvin, therefore, a phalanx of scholars rose up to defend the authority of Scripture in the face of scientific progress and in the climate of religious controversy after the Reformation, and a number of maps were elaborated in the continuing search for the exact location of paradise. The Dutch clergyman, cartographer and scholar Peter Plancius, for instance, created a map of paradise for the set of maps he had designed for Dutch Bibles from 1590 onwards (Fig 69). Plancius placed the locality of *Heden* and the vignette with Adam and Eve west of the single river, in Chaldaea, the region bordering Mesopotamia to the south east, with the Euphrates forming the boundary.

Degrees of latitude and longitude are indicated along the borders of the map, and two scale bars were provided for the measurement of distance – in 'German miles' (a traditional unit of measurement abandoned in the nineteenth century) and hours. Paradise, it is clear, was to be measured in the mathematically accurate terms of Ptolemaic geography. Thus, according to Plancius, Eden stretched from east to west for about 20 miles and was situated at approximately 34 degrees north and 80 degrees east.

The discovery of the site of paradise, in the eyes of early modern biblical scholars, depended on the disclosure of the real meaning of a Genesis text that had been corrupted over time by changes in the human and natural world since the Fall. The text of the Bible was scrutinised, above all by scholars of Hebrew language and culture, for clues to the geographical mystery of Eden that would allow it to be mapped. Traces of Eden were thought to be discernible in place names inherited from ancient civilisations, albeit in distorted form as a result of the confusion of languages at

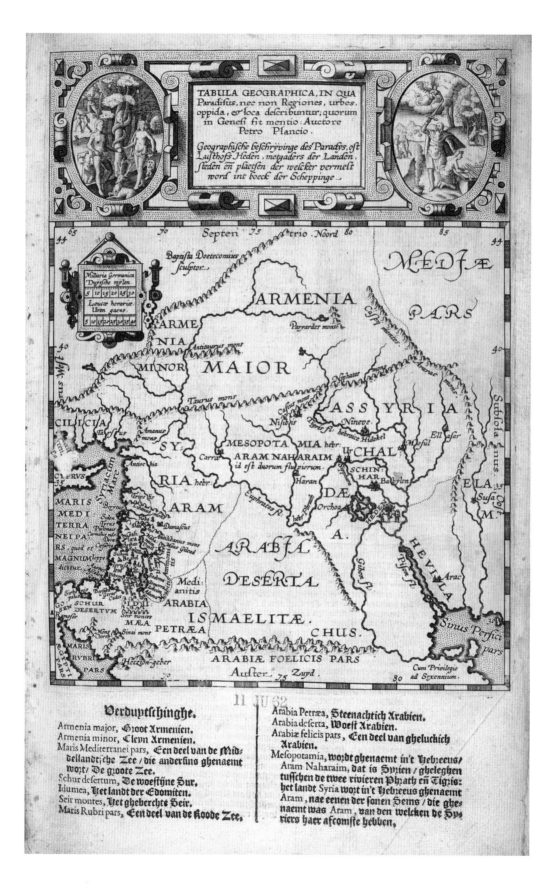

Fig 69 (opposite) *Peter Plancius's* Tabula geographica, in qua paradisus, nec non regiones, urbes, oppida, et loca describuntur... *for the beginning of Genesis, from a Protestant Dutch Bible (Amsterdam–Haarlem: Jacobszoon–Rooman, 1590). London, British Library, 3041.b.12.*

Fig 70 (right) *Map of the vast region of paradise (labelled* Paradisus)*, from Matthaeus Beroaldus,* Chronicum, Scripturae Sacrae autoritate constitutum *(Geneva: A. Chuppinus, 1575), p.88. London, British Library, C.79.e.12(1).*

Babel. The key to finding the location of paradise, the Calvinist Matthaeus Beroaldus (Matthieu Beroalde or Bérould) explained, was to appreciate that in the original Hebrew text of the Book of Genesis nouns may be singular in form but plural in meaning, for example when the vegetation and the trees are mentioned in Genesis 1.12 and 3.8. Thus the real sense of the statement found in Genesis, 'and a river went out of Eden to water paradise', was actually that 'rivers went out of Eden to water paradise'. Accordingly Beroaldus's map portrays four rivers flowing through paradise, shown as a huge region, populated by exotic animals; in the middle of it are represented Adam and Eve (Fig 70).

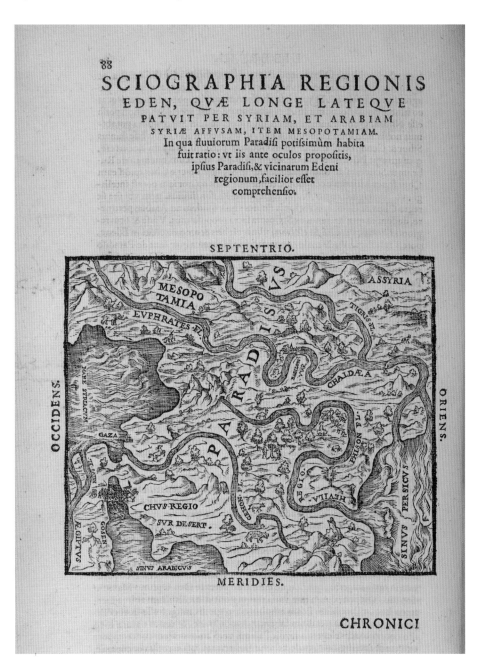

The map Beroaldus drew differed from Calvin's model of the four rivers of paradise, but it was an isolated case: Calvin's map had established the new model for the cartography of the earthly paradise. It must be noted, though, that some exegetes replaced Calvin's notion of two streams joining into a single river before branching again towards their mouths by the idea of four branches separating from a single river and continuing individually in the natural direction of flow – that is, from north to south. In this refined model, the single river was identified with the Euphrates and the branching streams with the dense network of tributaries in the Babylonian region. The Gihon and the Pison, which Calvin had identified with the lowest reaches of the Euphrates and the Tigris just above where they empty into the Persian Gulf, were now incorporated into the Mesopotamian river network.

This was the idea of the humanist and Protestant theologian Franciscus Iunius (François du Jon) and the orientalist Iohannes Hopkinsonus (John Hopkinson). Hopkinsonus's map shows a vignette with the figures of Adam and Eve and the Tree of Knowledge marking the site of paradise in the eastern part of the region of Eden,

Fig 71 (above) Ioannes Hopkinsonus (John Hopkinson), map of paradise, from his Synopsis paradisi, sive paradisi descriptio, ex variis ... scriptoribus desumpta, cum chorographica ... tabula (Leiden: Plantinus, 1593), final page. London, British Library, 570.f.1(1).

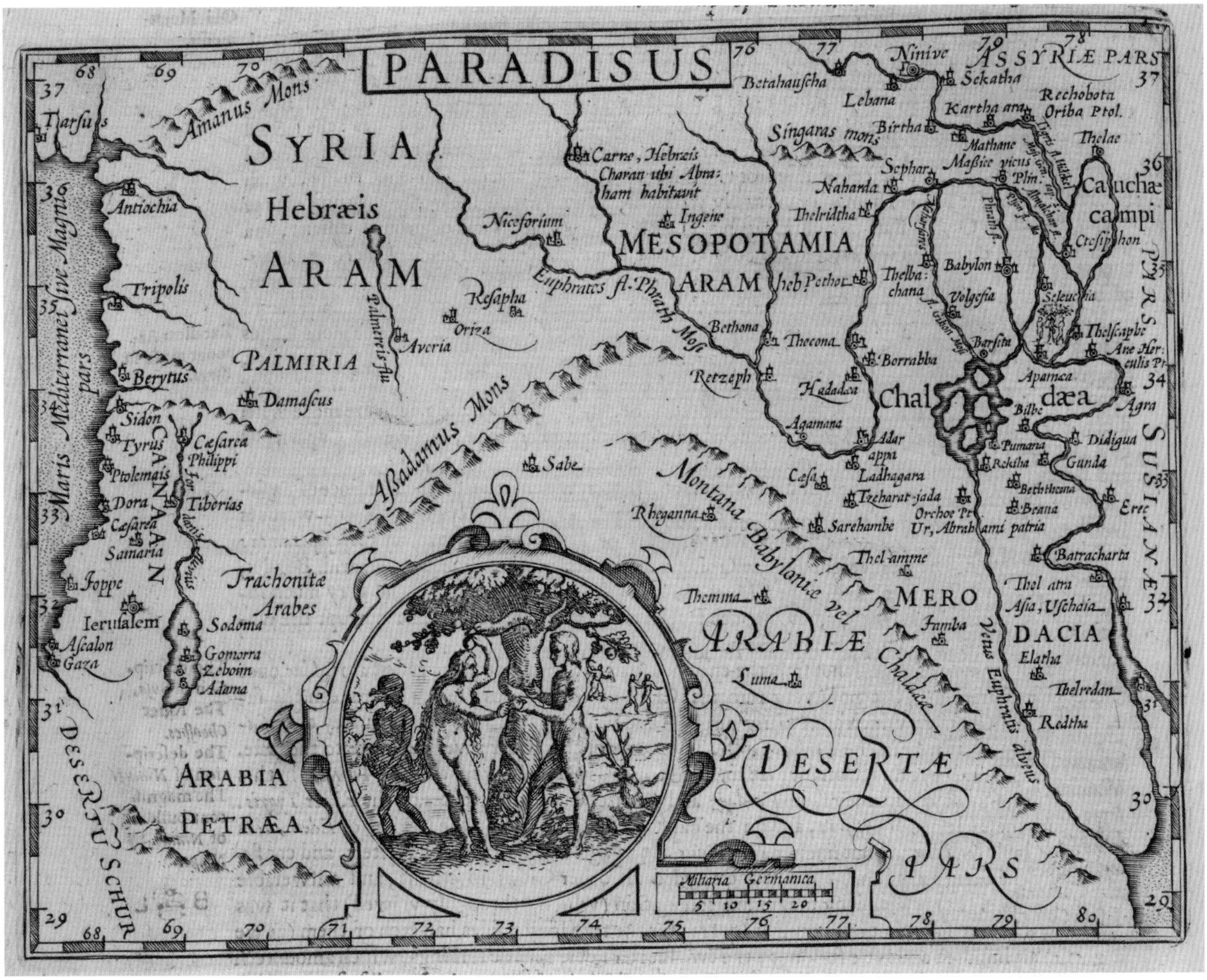
PARADISUS
SYRIA
Hebræis
ARAM
MESOPOTAMIA
ARAM
PALMIRIA
Damascus
Chal
dæa
ASSYRIÆ PARS
Ninive
Babylon
Seleucia
Apamea
Euphrates fl.
Amanus Mons
Antiochia
Tripolis
Berytus
Sidon
Tyrus
Tiberias
Ioppe
Ierusalem
Ascalon
Gaza
Sodoma
Gomorra
Adama
Trachonitæ
Arabes
ARABIA
PETRÆA
ARABIÆ
DESERTÆ
PARS
MERO
DACIA
Montana Babyloniæ vel Chaldææ
Maris Mediterranei sive Magnis pars
Vetus Euphratis alveus
Miliaria Germanica

Fig 72 (above) *Iodocus Hondius,* Paradisus, *from Gerard Mercator and Iodocus Hondius,* Atlas Minor *(Amsterdam: Iodocus Hondius, 1607/1610). London, British Library, Maps C.3.a.3.*

Fig 73 (overleaf) *Sir Walter Ralegh, map of paradise, from his* History of the World, *2nd edn (London: William Jaggard for Walter Burre, 1617), between pp.56–7. London, British Library, C.115.h.5.*

between the ancient cities of Apamea and Seleucia (Fig 71). A similar cartography of paradise was adopted in the early seventeenth century by the Flemish cartographer and engraver Iodocus Hondius (Fig 72), and by the English courtier, explorer and writer Sir Walter Ralegh (Fig 73).

After Ralegh, however, the notion of the four rivers as four branches separating off from the Euphrates was abandoned. Instead, preference was given to Calvin's idea that the four rivers corresponded to the Tigris and Euphrates (to the north of a Mesopotamian paradise) and to the Gihon and the Pison (to the south). At the end of the seventeenth century both the French Protestant clergyman Samuel Bochart and his friend and disciple Pierre-Daniel Huet, the Catholic bishop of Avranches, France, developed and refined Calvin's ideas about the mapping of Eden. Both placed the garden beside the single river formed from the confluence of the Tigris and Euphrates, and both reversed the Pison and the Gihon, naming the Gihon as the easternmost of the two streams into which the single river eventually divided. What we see in Bochart's map is the confluence of the rivers Tigris and Euphrates and a

CAPADOCIÆ PARS

ARMEN

CILICIÆ PARS

E dessa

Tarsus Adana

Mallus

Mara

CYRRESTICA

Issus

Sinus Issicus
or Alexandretta

Alexandretta

Aleppo or Hierapolis

Antiochia

CHALCIDICI

M

CYPRVS

Laodicia

Apamia

Adada

THE
MEDITE-

Aradus

Antaradus

CATANY

RAN

Tripolis

Botris

Palmyra

PALMYRENA

Byblus

Berytus

Archis

Libanus

Sidon

COELESYRIA

Alsadamus

THE DESE
PALMER

SEA

Tyre

Antelibanum

Damascus

Berathi

Cæsaria
philippi

Saue. or Saba

pte. Acon

Machati

Syria
Soba

SACCEA

Gessuri

BATANEA

ARABIA
AGRÆI

Cæsaria p.

Bassan

Sichem

Amorites

Ioppe

Bethel

Hai

Ammonites

MARTENI

IERVSALEM

Moabites

Aurana

Ascalon

ARABIA

AGVBENI

Midianites

PETREA

Idumites

Petra deserti

THE GREA

Pharan desart

OF A

Amalekites

Ismalites

THE RED SEA

ARABIA THE HAPPIE

Derbeta

DORBETA or MOSEL.

Hasanscyha

HASANSEPHA

SIBIS

The Isle of EDEN or Gezerta

Tyrus fl.

Caprus fl.

Gorgus fl.

Ain

Rechoboth

SINGARVS M.

O P O T A M I A

Thelbe Mancane

or Baldac

SIPPHARA or SEPHAR

Chalne or Seleuia yth: u m tie l

Hiddekel

Hiddekel

TELASER or THILVTHA

EVPHRATES

Gehon

Achad after ward. Auchanites

BABYLON

Ctesiphon

R.HESIPHA once RETSEPH

Strath

GEHON

PISON

Apamia

Herculis Aræ

TIGRIS

The first plantation of Chus.

HAVILA

EREC or ARACCA

The Arabians ÆSITÆ

Chuduca sumetime Chusea

Themna

CHALDEA

The lakes of Chaldea

MASSANI

VR or VRCHOA the habitation of Abraham

ER T

ER T

Teredon now Balsara

A

The auntient outlet of Geon now defolute into the lakes of Chaldea.

Calathua

The Arabians ORCHENI

R.aama

THE

PERSIAN

SEA

Sheba

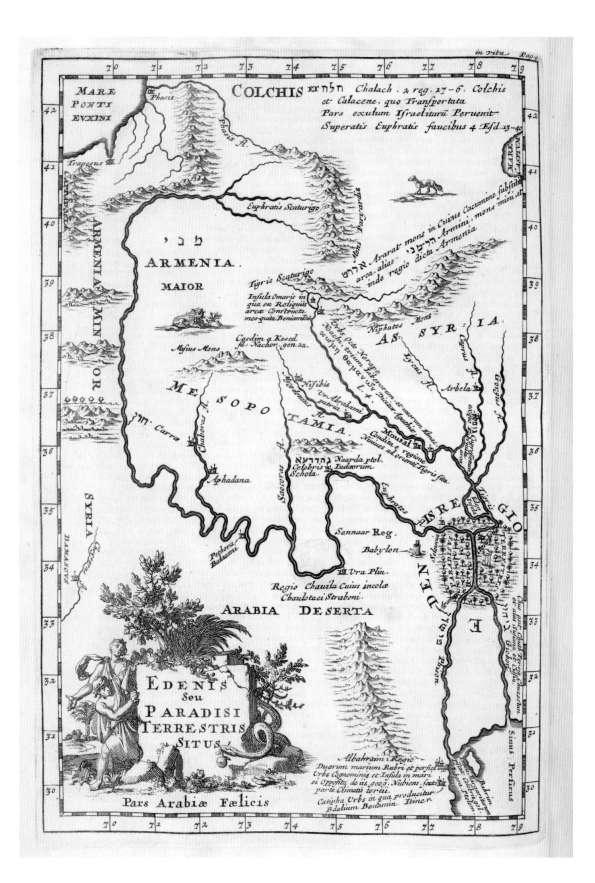

Fig 74 (opposite) *Samuel Bochart,* Edenis seu paradisi terrestris situs, *in* Opera omnia, *ed Stephanus Morinus (Étienne Morin) (Leiden: Cornelius Boutesteyn et Iordanus Luchtmans, 1692), p.9. London, British Library, 7.f.6.

Fig 74 (opposite) *Samuel Bochart,* Edenis seu paradisi terrestris situs, *in* Opera omnia, *ed Stephanus Morinus (Étienne Morin) (Leiden: Cornelius Boutesteyn et Iordanus Luchtmans, 1692), p.9. London, British Library, 7.f.6.*

Fig 75 (right) *Pierre-Daniel Huet,* A Map of the Situation of the Terrestrial Paradise, *from his* A Treatise of the Situation of the Terrestrial Paradise, *English translation by Thomas Gale (London: James Knapton, 1694), folded to face p.1. London, British Library, 1017.e.21.*

vast wooded region labelled *Paradisus terrestris*. The encircling words *Edenis regio* define a region that includes the cities of Babylon, Seleucia and Apamea (Fig 74). Huet, in his map, situated paradise on both sides of the single river formed by the junction of the Tigris and Euphrates, as Bochart did, but placed it on the southern arm of the bend made by the single river south of Babylonia (Figs 75 and 76). The validity of Huet's rather southerly siting of paradise was confirmed, in his view, by reports of the area's outstanding beauty and natural wealth – a relic of its original state and former blessedness.

In 1701, a few years after Huet placed the Garden of Eden unusually far south in Mesopotamia, the Dutch Reformed theologian Salomon Van Til gave it an unusually northern location (Fig 77). He suggested that the single river (marked on his map as *flumen Eden*) was the stream that the locals called *Odeines* (a derivation of the name *Eden*). It flowed in a straight course through paradise (*Hortus Dei*, or 'Garden of God')

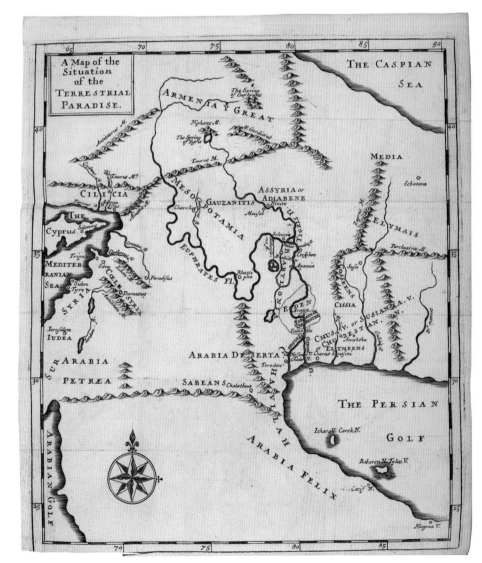

Fig 76 (left) *Pierre-Daniel Huet, map of paradise, frontispiece of his* Traité de la situation du paradis terrestre *(Paris: Jean Anisson, 1691). London, British Library, 219.c.15.*

before sending out branches east and west to the Tigris and the Euphrates, and then parting again into the Gihon and the Pison.

One of the few Catholic writers on the subject of the earthly paradise to follow Calvin and to attempt to show its location by means of a map was the German Jesuit scholar Athanasius Kircher. In his *Arca Noë* (1675), where he analysed all aspects relating to Noah's Ark, Kircher devoted a chapter to the issue 'whether the earthly paradise was destroyed by the Flood and in what place it was'. He adopted Luther's thesis that the Flood had devastated the earth, altering the courses of all rivers including those of paradise, and accepted Calvin's placement of the Garden of Eden in Mesopotamia. We are shown on Kircher's highly original map both prediluvian and postdiluvian rivers, the event of the Fall itself, Adam and Eve living as farmers

Fig 77 (right) *Salomon Van Til,* Tabula situm paradisi et regionum vicinarum referens, *from his* Dissertatio singularis geographico- theologica de situ paradisi terrestris, *in* Malachius illustratus *(Leiden: Iordanus Luchtmans, 1701), folded to face p.1. London, British Library, 854.h.23..*

away from the garden from which they had been banished, the sacrifice of Abel, his murder by Cain, the city of Enoch and the landing of the Ark on Mount Ararat (Fig 78). A square Garden of Eden and its internal details are prominently portrayed in bird's-eye perspective in the centre of the map.

In his chapter Kircher explained that the antediluvian spring in the middle of paradise had drawn its abundant waters from a huge underground reservoir in the mountains of Armenia. He believed that the four rivers had originally flowed out from it separately, one to each cardinal direction, watering first paradise itself and then, beyond the garden, the lands of Havilah, Cush and Assyria. After the Fall, however, God caused the spring to be blocked up so that its waters were forced back into the Armenian reservoir, from which they resurfaced in different parts of Armenia to give rise to the present river network. After this post-lapsarian change, Kircher maintained, the single source in paradise disappeared and nobody, not even the first Patriarchs, had ever been able to see it. The earthly paradise had vanished from Mesopotamia.

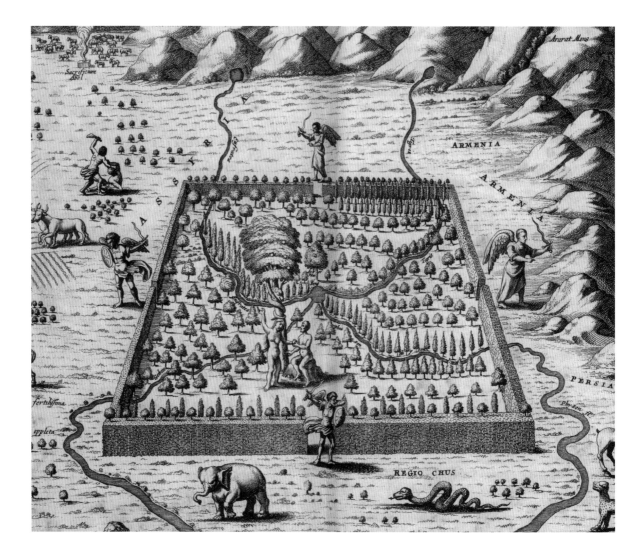

PARADISE IN ARMENIA AND THE HOLY LAND

Towards the end of the sixteenth century scholars accepted the fundamental elements of Calvin's brilliant exegetical solution: the Flood had wiped out a highly localised paradise within the region of Eden and, since the rivers were still there, the former site of paradise could be indicated on a map. Some exegetes, however, found it more appealing to search for paradise not in Mesopotamia (Steuchus's and Calvin's idea), but in Armenia – a region that in the sixteenth century included the area between the upper Euphrates and Lake Urmia, the Black Sea and the Syrian desert. Sound reasons could be found for this change of focus, not the least of which was that the identity of two of the four rivers named in Genesis, the Tigris and the Euphrates, was uncontroversial, and both rivers were known to rise in Armenia. Once scholarly attention had shifted northwards, the reasoning went, the more problematical Gihon and Pison were sure to be identified among the local rivers. Moreover, Noah's Ark had landed there; the region was well watered by rivers and had been praised for its fertility by the ancient authorities; and many Armenian place names included an element derived from the name 'Eden'.

In 1666 Marmaduke Carver, a Yorkshire parson, produced a map showing the single river of paradise rising in Greater Armenia, watering the garden and then dividing into four streams (Fig 79). About 60 years later, the distinguished French exegete Augustin Calmet drew a map, the *Carte du Paradis Terrestre* (1724–6), for the

Fig 78 (opposite and overleaf) *Athanasius Kircher's map* Topographia paradisi terrestris iuxta mentem et coniecturas authoris, *from his* Arca Noë *(Amsterdam: Ianssonius, 1675), between pp.196–7. London, British Library, 460.c.9.*

Fig 79 (right) *Marmaduke Carver's map of paradise, from his* A Discourse of the Terrestrial Paradise Aiming at a More Probable Discovery of The True Situation of that Happy Place of our First Parents Habitation *(London: James Flesher, 1666), after p.167. London, British Library, 4375.aa.12.*

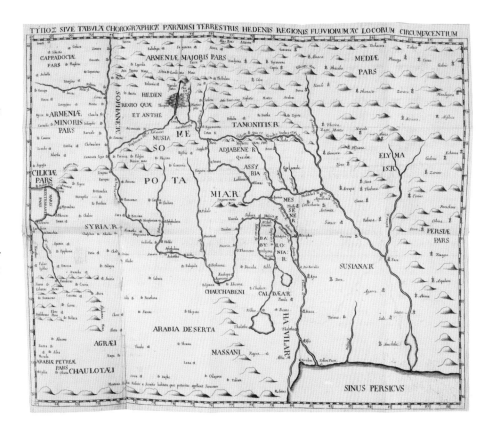

Mons

Liba-   nus.

Sacrificium
Abel.

Sacrificium
Kain

A S S Y R I A

Euphrates

Henochia Civitas primes
Gigantum à Kain excita.

Desertum   Pharan   et   SUR   olim fertilissima.

post Diluvium arenis oppleta

Sinai

Mons.

GEHON. FL.

Mare
Rubrum

ÆTIOPIA   ORIENTALIS

TERRA CHUS.

S AUTHORIS.

Avarat Mons

ARMENIA

ARMENIA

Tigris

Indus

GIO CHUS

SIVE SINUS

PERSICUS.

PERSIA

Physon fl.

ÆLAMITÆ

HEVILA REGIO

Ex tot tantisq̃ Regionibus, quas cælum suo ambitu
continet, hanc præsentem Paradisi terrestris Topographiam
quam et Edeniam regionem appello, tantis laudibus sacri Geo-
graphi omnes extollunt, ut communi omnium sententia, cæteras
omnes bonitate terræ, ubertate frugum, omnisq̃ generis
deliciis etiamnum longe antecellat, ut proinde Paradisus hîc
a Deo plantatus nonnullas pristinæ suæ felicitatis notas
reliquisse videatur, cujus situm et topographiam hîc præcise
juxta Sacræ Geneseos c. 2. v. 8. et 10. verba oculis præ-
pono curiosi Lectoris. Hortum itaq̃ voluptatis primò ponimus sub
quadrata figura, quasi typum cælestis Paradisi seu civi-
tatis in quadro juxta Apocalypseos descriptionem positæ;
Vides hîc pariter fontem seu fluvium, qui inde in quadru-
plicem mundi plagam divisus post Paradisi irrigationem
extra quoq̃ circumstas regiones Havila, Æthiopiam
orientalem, Terram Chus, Assyriam irrigat; Vides
quoq̃ arborem vitæ in medio Paradisi plantatam;
nec inde remotam arborem scientiæ boni et mali,
quæ causa sunt peccati in mundum introducti. Arborum
vero seriem non quod revera hunc situm habuerint;
sed qualem in horto voluptatis concipere licuit,
disposuimus. Extra vero Paradisum 4 Cherubiam
juxta paraphrasim chaldaicam (quos ipsa כרוביא
Cherubaia in plurali numero vocant) ad 4 mundi
partes disposito ad custodiendam viam ad lignum
vitæ flammeo versatiliq̃ gladio armatos consti-
tuimus. Deniq̃ extra Paradisum Adæ et Evæ
ex Paradiso expulsorum ærumnas et in agris
excolendis labores, et ex Cain fratricidæ afflicti-
ones exhibuimus; et similia, quæ ubi sat superq̃
expressa sunt, ita quoq̃ ulteriori expositione non
indigent, unde lector omnia scitus ex descriptione Paradisi,
intelliget. Vale fruere.

133

second edition of his biblical commentary. The map features the four rivers originally emanating from a single source (subsequently obliterated by the Flood and other natural disasters), rising close together in Armenia (Fig 80). Instead of a common source described by ancient writers, the Tigris and the Euphrates in Calmet's time sprang from different places within Armenia. The sources of the other two rivers of paradise were also in Armenia: the Pison corresponded to the River Phasis (which flowed into the Black Sea) and the Gihon to the River Araxes (which flowed into the Caspian Sea).

The arguments for a Mesopotamian or an Armenian paradise bear witness to the overall focus from the Renaissance onwards on the Middle East as the location

Fig 80 (below) *Augustin Calmet,* Carte du paradis terrestre, *from his* Commentaire littéral sur tous les livres de l'Ancien et du Nouveau Testament, *2nd edn, 8 vols (Paris: [n. pub.], 1724–6), I/1 (1724), folded to face p.20. London, British Library, 9.h.1.*

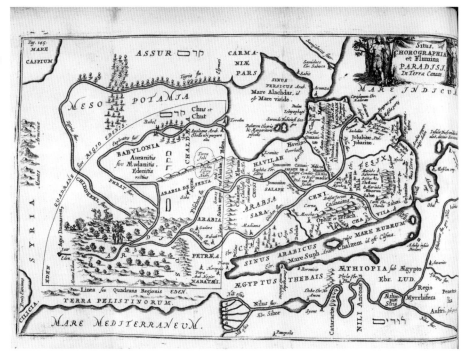

Fig 81 (right) *Iohannes Herbinius, Situs, chorographia et flumina paradisi in terra Canaan, from his* Dissertationes de admirandis mundi cataractis *(Amsterdam: Ianssonius, 1678), between pp.144–5. London, British Library, 233.i.27.*

of the earthly paradise. It is not surprising, thus, that many commentators, instead of looking at Mesopotamia or Armenia, found the temptation of making a case for a Holy Land paradise irresistible, since such a location carried the power of Christian salvation history. Situating Eden in Palestine meant identifying Adam's paradise not only with the Promised Land of the Old Testament, but also with the place where the Son of God (the Second Adam) had redeemed humankind from the consequences of Adam's Fall. In the final quarter of the seventeenth century, for example, the German-Polish naturalist Johannes Herbinius argued that the true place of paradise was the Holy Land, the country of the prophets, the Patriarchs and Christ. The map in his study of waterfalls, the *Dissertationes de admirandis mundi cataractis* (1678), was drawn to illustrate the idea that the biblical mention of paradise as planted from the east meant that the garden was not actually in Mesopotamia, but that it rather extended from the borders of Mesopotamia to the Land of Canaan (Fig 81). In Herbinius's view, the single river that had watered paradise was the River Jordan. On his map the Jordan's single underground source is placed to the north of the Lebanon mountains, and the river flows across paradise before separating outside it into the four branches.

The French Jesuit Jean Hardouin, author of a lengthy annotation of Pliny the Elder's *Natural History* (1685), added a treatise for the second edition of his work, published in 1723. This was accompanied by a double-folio map depicting the location of the earthly paradise (Fig 82). Hardouin intended to show how the biblical description of the Garden of Eden perfectly fitted Pliny's description of the geography of the Middle East. The division of the single river of paradise into four, he explained, referred not to its physical division, but to proportions. What the Genesis text meant

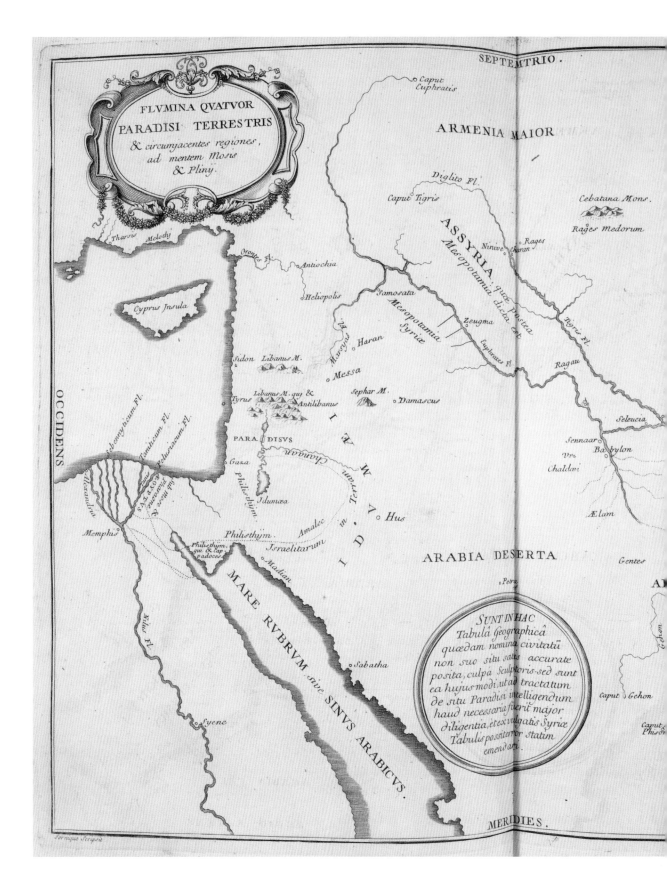

SEPTEMTRIO.

FLVMINA QVATVOR
PARADISI TERRESTRIS
& circumjacentes regiones,
ad mentem Mosis
& Plinÿ.

ARMENIA MAIOR

Caput
Euphratis

Diglito Fl.

Caput Tigris

Cebatana Mons.

Rages Medorum

ASSYRIA

Ninive · Rages
Charan

Tharsis   Melothy

Orontes Fl.

Antiochia

Mesopotamia quæ Postea

Heliopolis

Samosata

Mesopotamia
Syriæ

Zeugma

Tigris Fl.

Cyprus Insula

Euphrates Fl.

Ragau

Sidon Libanus M.

Marsyas Fl.

Haran

Tyrus

Messa

Sephar M.

Damascus

Seleucia

Libanus M. quj &
Antilibanus

PARADISVS

Chanaan

Sennaar

Vr

Babylon

Chaldæi

Gaza

Idumæa

Hus

Ælam

Schennyticum Fl.

Tanticum Fl.

Peluriacum Fl.

Alexandria

S. ALECT

Memphis

Philisthym.
qu & Cap
padoce

Philisthym

Israelitarum

Amalec

ARABIA DESERTA

Gentes

Madian

Petra

MARE   RVBRVM   sive   SINVS   ARABICVS.

Nilus Fl.

Sabatha

Caput Gehon

SVNT IN HAC
Tabulâ geographicâ
quædam nomina civitatū
non suo situ satis accurate
posita, culpâ Sculptoris·sed sunt
ea hujus modi, ut ad tractatum
de situ Paradisi intelligendum
haud necessaria fuerit major
diligentia, et ex vulgatis Syriæ
Tabulis possit error statim
emendari.

Syene

Caput
Phison

OCCIDENS

Fernaquis Scripsit

MERIDIES.

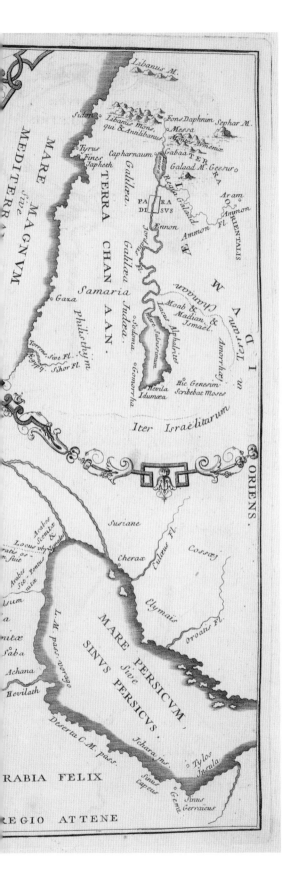

was that when paradise was compared with the lands that were watered by the four rivers, however fertile and wonderful each of these may have been, none had even a quarter of the beauty and perfection of the land that was watered by the single river. Even a quarter of the splendour of paradise far exceeded anything offered by Assyria (watered by the Tigris), Mesopotamia (watered by the Euphrates) or Cush and Havilah (watered by the Pison and the Gihon, both in Arabia Felix, the southern part of the Arabian peninsula, known in the ancient world to be wealthy and fertile, in Latin *felix*).

In Hardouin's ingenious reading of Genesis, the division of the rivers described in the text was no more than an expression of praise for the unimaginable quality of paradise. His map consistently shows the four rivers flowing to the Persian Gulf in one part of the Middle East and paradise placed in quite a different part, far away in the west, in the Holy Land. Paradise is described in greater detail in an inset at the top right of the map, where it is situated between Lake Genesareth and the Dead Sea, with the single river (the Jordan) flowing through it.

Linking the Garden of Eden and the land of the Crucifixion geographically, and cartographically, was a new way of expressing the old association between Adam and Christ. It was not only in nineteenth-century Sicily, where Garibaldi's Redshirts had landed and were pressing inland to overthrow the Kingdom of the Two Sicilies, that everything had to change to ensure that nothing had changed, as described in *Il Gattopardo*. In early modern Europe, the exegetical and cartographical context of the medieval belief in the Garden of Eden had to change so that the authority of Scripture could be fully maintained.

Fig 82 *Jean Hardouin's map of paradise, from his* De situ paradisi terrestris disquisitio, *in* Caii Plinii Secundi Historiae naturalis libri XXXVII, *2nd edn, 2 vols (Paris: Antonius–Urbanus Coustelier, 1723), I, between pp.358–9. London, British Library, 685.k.2.*

Visual Interlude
The Invisible Paradise in the Land of Canaan

◆

By the seventeenth century the identification of paradise with the Holy Land was an expression of a deeply felt spirituality that permitted a radical bending of geography in the interest of theology. In his *La Saincte Géographie* (1629) the aristocrat Jacques d'Auzoles, sieur de La Peyre, in Auvergne, France (commonly, if inaccurately, referred to as Lapeyre), argued that God had selected one particular place on earth as the site of the most important events of salvation history. He believed that Eden, the land of Adam's natural perfection and Fall, was the one and same land inhabited by Noah after the Flood, the land promised to Abraham and celebrated by the Prophets and, finally, the land of Christ. The Flood,

in Lapeyre's view, had had a huge impact on the configuration and landscape of the earth. Rather than a primordial single continent there were, by his day, four continents (those of the Old World and the Americas), together with the polar masses and numerous islands. Instead of a single sea surrounding the terrestrial landmass, there were several seas.

Lapeyre provided his readership with a cartographical analysis of the earth before and after the Flood. One of the maps included in his 1629 publication shows the region of Eden before the Flood: square in shape and containing a lozenge-shaped paradise (Fig 83). The western extremity of the Lebanon range (*Le mont Liban*) falls within

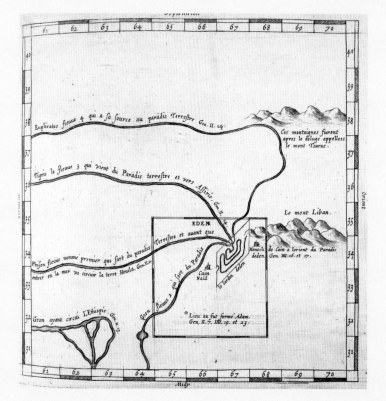

Fig 83 (left) *Jacques d'Auzoles Lapeyre, the antediluvian region of Eden, from his* La Saincte Géographie, c'est-à-dire, exacte description de la terre et veritable demonstration du paradis terrestre *(Paris: Antoine Estiene, 1629), p.91. London, British Library, 744.d.13.*

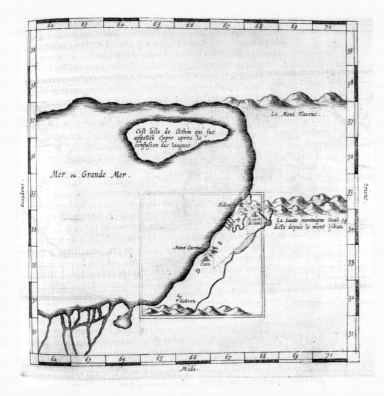

Fig 84 (left) *Jacques d'Auzoles Lapeyre,
the region of Eden after the Flood, from his*
La Saincte Géographie, c'est-à-dire,
exacte description de la terre et veritable
demonstration du paradis terrestre
*(Paris: Antoine Estiene, 1629), p.135.
London, British Library, 744.d.13.*

paradise, and from this the single river springs. It then follows a circuitous route through the garden, dividing into four just before emerging from paradise to flow out, first over Eden and then over the rest of the world. The mountains that would become the Taurus range are portrayed in the north, while the two cities of Enoch and Cain (the latter where Cain lived) flank paradise to east and west respectively. The place of Adam's creation is shown in the southern part of Eden.

Another map from Lapeyre's *La Saincte Géographie* depicts the same area after the Flood (Fig 84). From southern Anatolia to the delta of the Nile, the outline of the modern Mediterranean coast follows the course of the antediluvian rivers shown on the first map. The Taurus and the Lebanon ranges now terminate in the sea. South of the Lebanon range, the area of a lozenge-shaped paradise is indicated by a broken line. As on the map describing the lands surrounding paradise before the Flood, the region of Eden is contained within a square, but half of this is now occupied by the sea.

Taken together, the two maps (prediluvian and postdiluvian Eden) reveal the drama of the Flood. Once the northwestern half of the region has been submerged, the postdiluvian paradise appears to be located along the Mediterranean shore of the Land of Canaan. There is no sign of the four rivers of paradise that had featured so prominently on the earlier map. Before the Flood, the single river had divided into four at the site of what is now the city of Tyre (unmarked but south of Sidon), shown containing four springs. After the Flood, the waters of which inundated the northwestern part of the region of Eden, the four rivers have disappeared into the sea. The garden, Lapeyre explained, had been planted in the eastern part of the region of Eden, in the area now corresponding to Galilee, which had been left intact by the Flood. Paradise, therefore, was still there, where it had always been; the only change was in its visibility. Sin made paradise disappear from human sight, but with divine grace God may still open human eyes to see the Garden of Eden.

Bibliographic Essay

⸻ ◆ ⸻

On the historical atlas there is the wide-ranging study by Walter Goffart, *Historical Atlases: The First Three Hundred Years 1570–1870* (Chicago–London: University of Chicago Press, 2003). The phrase *Historiae oculus geographia* appears on the title page of the *Parergon* accompanying Ortelius's *Theatrum Orbis terrarum* (Antwerp: apud Christophorum Plantinum, 1584; ex officina Plantiniana, apud Ioannem Moretum, 1601). A treatment of sixteenth- and seventeenth-century regional maps of paradise is in Ute Kleinmann, 'Wo lag das Paradies? Beobachtungen zu den Paradieslandschaften des 16. und 17. Jahrhunderts', in *Die flämische Landschaft 1520–1700* (Lingen: Luca Verlag, 2003), pp.279–85 (illustrations, pp.286–303); and Cécile Kruyfhooft, 'Genesis 2, 10–14: De ligging van het paradijs', in Carl Van de Velde *et al*, *Het aards paradijs. Dierenvoorstellingen in de Nederlanden van de 16de en 17de eeuw* (Antwerp: Koninklijke Maatschappij voor Dierkunde van Antwerpen, 1982), pp.137–52.

A good and comprehensive survey of post sixteenth-century printed maps relating to the Bible is in Catherine Delano-Smith and Elizabeth M. Ingram, *Maps in Bibles, 1500–1600: An Illustrated Catalogue* (Geneva: Droz, 1991). See also Delano-Smith, 'Maps in Bibles in the sixteenth century', *The Map Collector*, 39 (1987), pp.2–14; Franco Motta, '*Geographia sacra*: il luogo del paradiso nella teologia francese del tardo Seicento', *Annali di Storia dell'Esegesi*, 14:2 (1997), pp.477–506; Claudine Poulouin, *Le Temps des origines. L'Eden, le Déluge et «les temps reculés». De Pascal à l'*Encyclopédie (Paris: Honoré Champion, 1998).

Mapmakers discussed in this chapter include Peter Plancius, whose *Tabula geographica* was inserted in a Protestant Dutch Bible (Amsterdam–Haarlem: Jacobszoon-Rooman, 1590) [the map is at the beginning of the Book of Genesis]; Matthaeus Beroaldus, *Chronicum, Scripturae Sacrae autoritate constitutum* (Geneva: Antonius Chuppinus, 1575) [his map is at the end of chapter 7, which is entitled *De paradiso*, pp.78–88]; Franciscus Iunius (François du Jon), *Praelectiones in Genesim* (Heidelberg: [n. publ.], 1589) [the map is before p.1]; Ioannes Hopkinsonus (John Hopkinson), *Synopsis paradisi sive paradisi descriptio* (Leiden: Plantinus, 1593) [the map is printed on the final page]; Iodocus Hondius, whose map of paradise was included in Gerard Mercator and Iodocus Hondius, *Atlas Minor* (Amsterdam: Iodocus Hondius, 1607; 1610); Sir Walter Ralegh, *History of the World*, 2nd edn (London: William Jaggard for Walter Burre, 1617) [the map is between pp.56–7]; Pierre-Daniel Huet, *Traité de la situation du paradis terrestre* (Paris: Jean Anisson, 1691), Thomas Gale, trans.: *A Treatise of the Situation of the Terrestrial Paradise* (London: James Knapton, 1694); Salomon Van Til, *Dissertatio singularis geographico-theologica de situ paradisi terrestris*, in *Malachius illustratus* (Leiden: Iordanus Luchtmans, 1701); Athanasius Kircher, *Arca Noë, in tres libro digesta* (Amsterdam: Ioannes Iannsonius, 1675), pp.22–186; Marmaduke Carver, *A Discourse of the Terrestrial Paradise Aiming At a More Probable Discovery of The Trye Situation of That Happy Place of our First Parents Habitation* (London: James Flesher, 1666); Jean Hardouin, *De situ paradisi terrestris disquisitio*, in *Caii Plinii Secundi Historiae naturalis libri XXXVII*, 2nd edn, 2 vols (Paris: Antonius-Urbanus Coustelier, 1723), I, pp.359–68 [Hardouin's five-volume edition of the Elder Pliny's *Natural History* made him famous]; Jacques d'Auzoles Lapeyre, *La Saincte Géographie, c'est-à-dire, exacte description de la terre et veritable demonstration du paradis terrestre* (Paris: Antoine Estiene, 1629).

Samuel Bochart's manuscript notes on the

location of paradise are in the Bibliothèque Municipale, Caen and Paris; his treatise was included in his collected works, the posthumous *Opera omnia*, edited and published in 1692 by his biographer and disciple Étienne Morin. Augustin Calmet's comments on paradise are in his *Commentaire littéral sur tous les livres de l'Ancien et du Nouveau Testament*, 2nd edn, 8 vols (Paris: [n. publ.], 1724–6), I/1 (1724), pp.20–9. Iohannes Herbinius's tract on paradise is found in his *Dissertationes de admirandis mundi cataractis* (Amsterdam: Ioannes Ianssonius, 1678), pp.136–88.

On Ortelius's historical maps in general see Peter H. Meurer, 'Ortelius as the Father of Historical Cartography', in Marcel van den Broecke, Peter Van der Krogt and Peter H. Meurer, eds., *Abraham Ortelius and the First Atlas. Essays Commemorating the Quadricentennial of his Death, 1598–1998* (Houten, The Netherlands: HES, 1998), pp.133–59.

On Huet see April G. Shelford, *Faith and Glory: Pierre-Daniel Huet and the Making of the Demonstratio Evangelica (1679)*, PhD. dissertation, Princeton University, 1997; Elena Rapetti, *Pierre-Daniel Huet: erudizione, filosofia, apologetica* (Milan: Vita e Pensiero, 1999); Jean-Robert Massimi, 'Montrer et démontrer: autour du *Traité de la situation du paradis terrestre* de P. D. Huet (1691)', in Alain Desrumeaux and Francis Schmidt, eds., *Moïse géographe. Recherches sur les représentations juives et chrétiennes de l'espace* (Paris: Vrin, 1988), pp.203–25.

On Kircher see Janet Brown, 'Noah's Flood, the Ark, and the Shaping of Early Modern Natural History', in David C. Lindberg and Ronald L. Numbers, eds., *When Science and Christianity Meet* (Chicago–London: The University of Chicago Press, 2003) pp.115–17; Denis Cosgrove,

'Global Illumination and Enlightenment in the Geographies of Vincenzo Coronelli and Athanasius Kircher', in David N. Livingstone and Charles W. J. Withers, eds., *Geography and Enlightenment* (Chicago–London: University of Chicago Press, 1999), pp.33–66.

Fig 85 (below) *Athanasius Kircher's map* Topographia paradisi terrestris iuxta mentem et coniecturas authoris, *from his* Arca Noë *(Amsterdam: Ianssonius, 1675), between pp.196–7. London, British Library, 460.c.9. Detail of Fig 78: the original sin of Adam and Eve.*

CHAPTER 8

NEW LIFE INTO AN OLD DEBATE

Once upon a time there was a king's son; nobody in the world had a larger and more beautiful collection of books than he did. In this collection he could read and see, depicted in splendid engravings, information about every people of every land. But as to where the Garden of Eden was, he could not find a single word; yet it was just this on which he meditated most of all.

One day, as he was walking alone in the wood, a storm obliged him to find refuge in a large cave that turned out to be the Cavern of the Winds. There the East Wind, dressed like a Chinese, agreed to carry him to the garden of paradise. After flying high up and very fast above the clouds, they finally entered the island of happiness, in which that delicious garden bloomed.

FROM *THE GARDEN OF PARADISE*
BY HANS CHRISTIAN ANDERSEN, 1838

SECULAR SCHOLARS SEARCHING FOR EDEN

In Andersen's fairy tale, the East Wind deposited the prince in a magnificent garden, where flowers and leaves sang the sweet songs of his childhood. Then the young and beautiful fairy of paradise appeared to lead the prince by the hand to her splendid palace. The prince was delighted, but, despite the fairy's warnings, he could not resist the temptation of kissing her lips, with the result that the garden of paradise immediately sank deep into the earth and was lost. In 1885 William Fairfield Warren, in a book in which he located paradise at the North Pole, referred to Andersen's fairy tale. Warren's aim, however, was not to express regret over another loss of paradise by human disobedience. It was to point out that great interest in its location was still alive in his day.

Andersen's prince could read and see in his many beautiful books all that had ever happened in the world. Yet he was still tormented with a consuming curiosity because his great library contained no information as to where the Garden of Eden might be. In the same way, Warren claimed, the more the modern world had advanced in new knowledge the more urgent became the need to find a solution to the issue of paradise's whereabouts. As he put it, 'the lapse of centuries has rendered many another question antiquated, but not this'. Warren noted that a wide range of scholars and intellectuals of his day – historians, archaeologists, paleontological anthropologists, mythographers, theologians and sociologists – were all seeking to determine the starting point of human history, and to shed light upon the geographical cradle of the human race.

What is remarkable is that by the nineteenth century, whereas Christian theologians belonging to mainstream denominations had given up the search for the location of Eden, secular scholars, fringe exegetes and others had picked up the task of plotting the precise original site of humankind. Even at the end of the eighteenth century, the question of paradise's location was already presented to Bible readers as an irresolvable and, in the final analysis, not particularly important puzzle. Paul Wright's *New Map of the Garden and Land of Eden*, compiled for the *Family Bible* that he published in London in 1782, provided a cartographical synthesis of the principal ideas about the location of paradise that had been expounded between the sixteenth and the eighteenth centuries (Fig 86). Eden is hinted at with hatched, oval-shaped circles both in Armenia (at the top of the map) and Mesopotamia (at the bottom), while a note (just below the compass, on the right) points out that another possible site for Eden is near the Holy Land. The map also illustrates the theory that paradise had once been situated in an area now entirely covered by the sea. The author of the map clearly had recognised the wide-ranging debate over paradise's location. The continuous multiplication of theories and maps from the sixteenth century onwards had made it increasingly obvious that a single, authoritative solution to the question would never be found. This negative conclusion was not, however, perceived as a disaster.

From the nineteenth century onwards it was no longer considered a vitally urgent matter whether the Garden of Eden had been situated in Armenia, Mesopotamia or

Previous page: Paradise in the Middle East, *according to the Jehovah's Witnesses's publication* From Paradise Lost to Paradise Regained *(Brooklyn, NY: Watchtower Bible and Tract Society of New York, 1958), endpapers. Detail: the Fall and other biblical events.*

Fig 86 (opposite) *Paul Wright, New Map of the Garden and Land of Eden, in Wright, ed, The Complete British Family Bible (London: for Alex Hogg, 1782). London, British Library, L.15.d.7.*

New
MAP
OF
THE GARDEN
AND LAND
OF
EDEN
&c.

ARMENIA

Mt. Niphates
L. Thospitis

Land of Eden,
according to Reland,
Calmet & Sansow.

Mt. Ararat
where the Ark rested

Mt. Gordyæi

CASPIAN SEA

R. Euphrates

Mt. Taurus

R. Tigris

ASSYRIA

MESOPOTAMIA

NINIVEH

R. GORGUS

MEDIA
ATROPATENE

Mt. Caspius

Ecbatana

MEDIA

Mt. Zagrus

LAND

OF

CHUSH

OR

Seleucia

Tower of
Babel
BABYLON

CHALDEA

EUPHRATES

ARABIA DESERTA

CHUSHES-

-TAN

MAJOR

LAND of EDEN
according to Calvin,
Bochart, Wells, Huet & Patrick.

R. GIHON OR TAB

N.B. Heidegger, Hardouin, & Le Clerc
suppose Eden to have been situated near Mt. Lebanon, in Syria.

Basra

PISON

Chader I.

R. TIGRIS or HIDDEKEL

LAND OF HAVILAH

R. EUPHRATES

R. EUPHRATES

Pearl fishery

PARA
DISE

LAND OF EDEN now
Persian Gulph

This situation of Eden is supported
by the opinion of several celebrated
Divines, who suppose that place &
parts adjacent to be now swallowed
up by the Persian Gulph.

Gulph of Ormus

Engraved for The Revd. Dr. Wright's Complete British Family Bible.

anywhere else. For centuries the Bible had been trusted implicitly as the word of God and as a document inspired in its entirety by the Holy Spirit. In the course of the eighteenth century the notion began to emerge that the text of Scripture was, like any other text, open to philological and historical enquiry, and that its production could be related to external circumstances. In the new historical-critical methodology (a logical, if extreme, development of the traditional literal and historical reading of Scripture), the Bible began to be analysed as separate units of text that represented different traditions. Biblical scholars began to accept that – although they still considered it as having been inspired by God – the Scriptural text they were reading might represent the work of different authors. The geographical references found in Genesis were now understood to reflect the individual knowledge of the ancient scholar who, while expressing ideas common in his day, had been inspired by God to convey principally moral teachings, rather than a geographical or even historical record. The deployment of cartography in the service of biblical exegesis was thus becoming unnecessary. The Bible was increasingly seen as a *religious* text, and no longer as the infallible depository of scientific theories.

Mainstream theologians seemed content to set aside any unresolved questions about paradise and to replace the heated debates of previous centuries about its location with debates that were no less warm but that concerned other matters, such as evolution, ecumenism, the Church's social doctrine, the reform of liturgy and modernism. They neither showed much concern over the location of the lost Garden of Eden nor invested their intellectual energies in trying to create cartographical evidence to corroborate the Scriptures. They had bigger fish to fry. For Catholics and Protestants alike, the latitude and longitude of the Garden of Eden were no longer needed to validate the authority of the Scriptures in support of the Christian faith. Most Christian theologians today also prefer to stress the symbolic meaning of the paradise narrative, even when they accept its historical validity (not all do). Rather than argue over the exact site of the Garden of Eden, they describe paradise as the state of human perfection that was lost through sin. To them the paradise story is true in the sense that it presents, in a figurative style that accommodated the understanding of an ancient Middle-Eastern audience, the two most important truths on which they base their striving for eternal salvation: the essential goodness of creation and the consequences of human disobedience.

The lack of engagement of theologians belonging to major Christian churches with the paradise question created a vacuum on the subject. And where biblical exegetes had fallen silent, a wide range of secular scholars were not shy of stepping into the breach. After well over a millennium of sober exegetical mapping by clerics and pastors, the earthly paradise was abandoned to the zeal of the non-professional enthusiast. Today, too, those who set themselves the task of mapping the location of the earthly paradise usually do so with the unbridled energy of a beginner who has little if anything to do with mainstream theology.

BABYLON AND THE BIBLE

The gap left by the fading interest of professional theologians, who had ceased to question the site of an earthly paradise and whose minds had turned to other matters, happened to coincide in the nineteenth century with breathtaking archaeological discoveries. These came from the excavation of ancient sites in the Middle East, such as Babylon, Nineveh, Nimrud, Persepolis, Ur and Eridu. Most crucial in the assessment of the new findings was the decipherment of the long-lost cuneiform writing system. This was made possible by the full transcription and translation of a trilingual inscription, carved around the end of the sixth century BC on the rock of Mount Behistun, in western Iran. The monumental relief, an account of battles and victories by the Persian emperor Darius the Great, had been written in Old Persian (possibly invented upon Darius's instruction as an artificial cuneiform script intended specifically for royal monumental inscriptions and used from the sixth to the fourth century BC), Elamite (the language written in present-day Iran from the third to the first millennium BC) and Babylonian (a dialect of Akkadian, the Semitic language written in Mesopotamia also from the third to the first millennium BC).

The untiring efforts of field and armchair archaeologists, philologists and students of ancient texts and artefacts were shedding new light on the astonishing importance of Mesopotamian culture in the ancient world. The Old Testament could now be – indeed, had to be – seen completely differently. Western Christian societies were accustomed to a vision of their past as based uniquely on Graeco-Roman classical traditions; now the notion emerged that their Holy Scriptures came from ancient and largely unknown Middle Eastern civilisations. A growing number of specialists in every aspect of the past in Mesopotamia were keen to show how ancient Hebrew and Middle Eastern ideas, legends and myths were shared, and how the biblical world view depended on ancient Babylonian culture. Scholars of Middle Eastern ethnography, literature and religion created a cartography of a Babylonian Garden of Eden. New life was being poured into an old debate, which had seemed to have reached stalemate and to be on the verge of drying up.

In 1849 Sir Austen Henry Layard, English diplomat and archaeologist, suggested that there was a direct connection between mural bas-reliefs in the Assyrian palace at Nimrud, depicting what he described as a 'sacred tree', and the Tree of Life refered to in Genesis. In 1881 German scholar Friedrich Delitzsch claimed that an Akkadian tablet listed the Babylonian equivalent of the biblical paradise. He interpreted a passage, in which he recognised the Sumerian word *edin*, as identical with the Garden of Eden of Genesis. On his map of a Babylonian Garden of Eden, Delitzsch showed Babylonia at the time of the Assyro-Babylonian empire, identifying Cush with the land of the Kassites (Kassu) and Havilah with a region in southern Mesopotamia. Paradise is located on the Euphrates between Baghdad and Babylon (Fig 87).

A contemporary of Delitzsch, Archibald Henry Sayce, Oxford professor of Assyriology (the study of ancient Mesopotamia), had actually never travelled in Mesopotamia (unlike Delitzsch). But, like Delitzsch, he located there the Genesis

Fig 87 (overleaf) *Friedrich Delitzsch's map of Babylon, showing the Garden of Eden, from his book* Wo lag das Paradies? *(Leipzig: J.C. Hinrich, 1881). London, British Library, 2200.bb.13.*

Karte
von
BABYLONIEN
zur Zeit des assyrischen und babylonischen Weltreichs
mit
besonderer Berücksichtigung
der
biblischen Landschaft
GAN EDEN ODER DES PARADIESES.
Nach Angabe des Prof. Friedr. Delitzsch
gezeichnet.

Jetziges Mündungsgebiet des Schatt el - Arab.

Persischer
Meerbusen

Gez. von Th.v.Bomsdorff.

Leipzig, I.C. Hinrichs' sche Buchhandlung.

Garden of Eden, with the Sumerian *edin*. The site was near the shrine city of Eridu, at the point where fresh river water meets the saltwater of the sea. In his view, the one river watering the Garden of Eden mentioned in the Bible was an allusion to the Persian Gulf borrowed from a Babylonian source. In a falling tide, the body of saltwater would have seemed to a Babylonian viewer to be flowing back out of the gulf into the rivers. In Babylonian seals depicting Ea, the god of *abzu* ('sweet water'), Sayce saw representations of the four rivers of paradise: the Tigris, the Euphrates, the Pishon and the Gihon, the latter two being ancient man-made canals running parallel to the Tigris and the Euphrates; all rivers flowed into the Persian Gulf from their springs in the north, or their 'heads' (*capita*, the Latin term in the Vulgate, already noticed by Calvin). Sayce considered the Persian Gulf, described in cuneiform texts as 'the Salt River', to be the source (in the sense of mouth) of the four rivers of Genesis.

Sayce published his writings and lectures around the same years Delitzsch made his claims, but their approach was completely different. For Sayce the discovery of Mesopotamian culture proved that the Bible was historically trustworthy. Significantly, one of his successful booklets was titled *Fresh Light from the Ancient Monuments: A Sketch of the Most Striking Confirmations of the Bible from Recent Discoveries in Egypt, Assyria, Palestine, Babylonia, Asia Minor* (1883). By contrast, Delitzsch's aim was to show how ancient Hebrew and Middle Eastern ideas, legends and myths were shared, and how the biblical world view depended on ancient Babylonian culture. It was not only the Genesis account of the Garden of Eden that could be traced to ancient Babylon. Delitzsch pointed to a Babylonian story of the world's creation, a Babylonian account of the Flood and an account of the Fall of man allegedly found on a Babylonian cylinder-seal. He also suggested that the ten antediluvian patriarchs recorded in the Bible were in fact Babylonian kings who reigned before the Flood. The thought that the Old Testament stories were of Babylonian origin dealt a fatal blow to the belief that everything in the Old Testament was original. More critically, it threatened belief in the text's divine inspiration. Not surprisingly, Delitzsch's thesis proved highly controversial.

Whether the findings of Assyrian and Babylonian antiquities were seen as threatening or demonstrating the truth of the biblical text, Layard, Delitzsch and Sayce were not alone in their interpretations: other historians and philologists also found representations of the Tree of Life of the Garden of Eden on Assyrian seals or on mural bas-reliefs. The importance of the ancient geography of Mesopotamia to the Book of Genesis was appreciated outside the academic circles as well. William Willcocks, a British engineer who was consultant to the Turkish government in the aftermath of the First World War, made use of his knowledge and practical experience of the techniques of irrigation to map the Mesopotamian sites of two paradises: a biblical Eden, near the cataracts north of the confluence of the Tigris and the Euphrates, and a Sumerian Eden, in the marshlands of the Persian Gulf.

By the 1950s, however, the attempt to map a Babylonian paradise had become unfashionable among Assyriologists. There were too many discrepancies between the biblical account and the picture that was emerging from the huge numbers of cuneiform texts that had been deciphered over the preceding half century. What had once been the mainstream approach in Assyriology became the occupation of a minority, from whom new claims for a southern Mesopotamian Eden continued to be made. As recently as 2002 German Assyriologist Manfred Dietrich revisited Sayce's theory from the nineteenth century that the site of the Garden of Eden was at Eridu, in southern Mesopotamia, where fresh river water met the saltwater of the sea.

A SWINGING PENDULUM

Trends in Assyrian studies have parallelled biblical studies, with the difference that in biblical exegesis the seesaw of opposing tendencies lasted for centuries rather than just decades. Ideas that today are held by a minority, and are considered at or close to the fringe, belonged yesterday to the mainstream. Nobody in the established Church today, either Catholic or Protestant, would ascribe major theological importance to the issue of the earthly paradise's location, let alone seek to indicate its site on a map. Attempts to locate paradise on a map are today viewed by theologians belonging to major Christian churches as the vain exercises of fringe and fundamentalist mavericks. Mainstream thinking in the past, however, was very different. A literal approach to the Bible has nearly always been an integral part of theological history, and we should not forget that the theology of profound intellects, such as St Augustine and Calvin, lies at the origin of modern biblical scholarship.

From the time of St Augustine onward, all those who placed the earthly paradise on a map of the world or indicated its location on a regional map, as Calvin did, were at the forefront of Christian thought. These scholars were – in their time and, in many cases, for centuries afterwards – accepted as leading authorities in Bible interpretation. Today it happens to be more fashionable to read the Bible for a symbolic message than it was at other times in the past; but from the early Middle Ages to the early modern period, throughout the whole span of centuries between Augustine and Calvin, the uncompromisingly symbolical stance set, for example, by Platonist commentators was disowned by leading exegetes. The tendency at such

Fig 88 Paradise in the Middle East, *according to the Jehovah's Witnesses's publication* From Paradise Lost to Paradise Regained *(Brooklyn, NY: Watchtower Bible and Tract Society of New York, 1958), endpapers. Detail: the Fall and other biblical events.*

times was to pair symbolic interpretations with the fringe and literal interpretations with the mainstream. Today the tendency in ecclesiastic and academic establishment thinking is to keep a guarded distance from those who insist on a literal interpretation of the narrative recorded in the Book of Genesis.

Yet while theologians, like the Assyriologists, have turned their backs firmly on the issue of paradise's location, maps purporting to demonstrate the former whereabouts of the Garden of Eden are still being published in the name of religion. Their authors come from groups who, like the Jehovah's Witnesses, adhere to a highly literal interpretation of the biblical text (Fig 88).

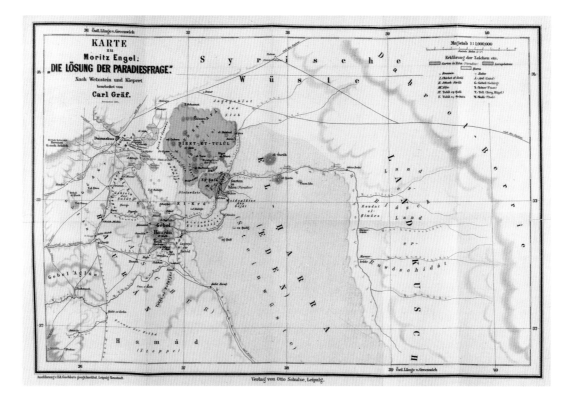

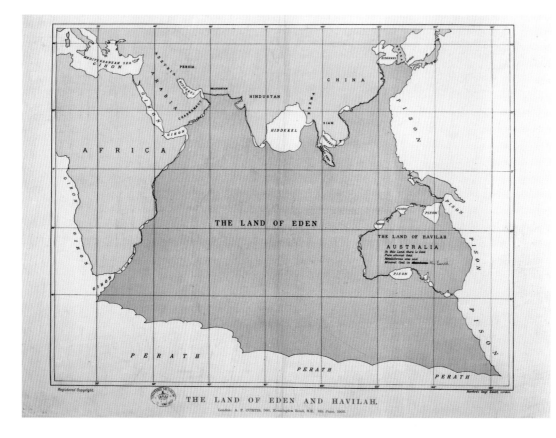

Many, if not most, nineteenth- and twentieth-century maps of the earthly paradise have come from the so-called intellectual fringe. Of all the locations for paradise suggested over the last five centuries, the confluence of the Tigris and the Euphrates has proved the most enduring. Other sites for paradise have been proposed, often echoing earlier theories. In 1885 Moritz Engel placed paradise in an oasis in the Syrian desert, at Ruhbe, east of Damascus (Fig 89). In 1905 A. P. Curtis, who printed a map called *The Land of Eden and Havilah*, clearly had in mind the early modern idea that before the Flood paradise existed on a very different-looking earth from that of modern times, so he showed on his map the antediluvian lands, later submerged by the Flood (Fig 90).

Other twentieth-century writers placed paradise in more familiar regions. It has been set in the Arabian desert by the Orientalist Albert Herrmann (1931) and, more recently, by Kamal Salibi (1996); in Mesopotamia by Richard Hennig (1950); in Armenia by Lars Ringbom, who even pointed to a specific plateau near the Caspian Sea (1958), and by David Rohl (1998). Others, giving a new twist to another earlier idea,

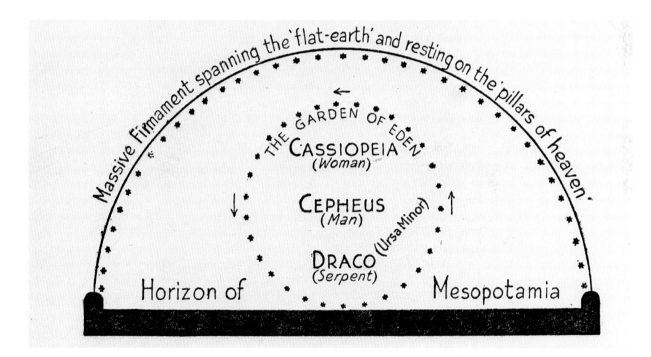

claimed that the earthly paradise was above the earth, in the heavenly sphere. Thus in 1935 James E. Nicholson dismissed the Garden of Eden as an invention elaborated by Jewish priests out of a Babylonian myth, insisting instead that it occupied the space within the circle of circumpolar stars when viewed from the latitude of Mesopotamia (Fig 91). Nicholson explained that the Expulsion represented the driving out of the Man (the constellation Cepheus) and the Woman (the constellation Cassiopeia) by the precession of the equinoxes. Both constellations are set to return in the future, in about 3,500 years.

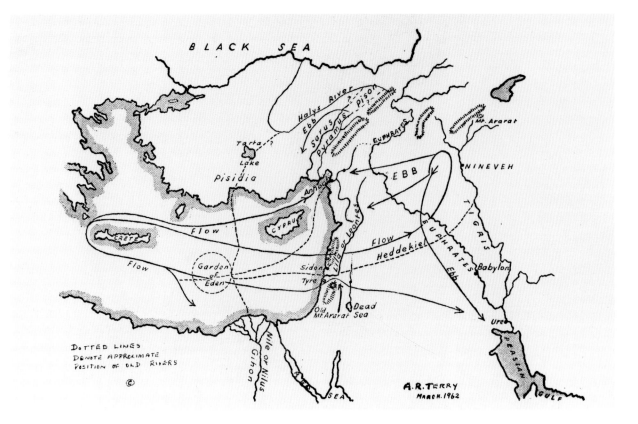

The idea of a submerged Eden also had its twentieth-century advocates. In 1962 the Baptist Albert R. Terry claimed to have received confirmation directly from God, through dreams and signs, that the site of Eden lay below the Mediterranean Sea (Fig 92). Then in 1998, right at the end of the second millennium, the not entirely novel claim that paradise had been at the centre of the world was posted on the internet. The proposed site was in the Delta of the River Nile, and thus exactly at the centre of the terrestrial land mass (including the Eurasian, African and American continents), at 32 degrees E, 32 degrees N. Three other papers produced between 2001 and 2005 have also been posted on the internet. All are by Emilio Spedicato, a mathematics lecturer from the University of Bergamo in northern Italy, who claims that the Garden of Eden was situated in the Hunza Valley in northern Pakistan, not far from the Pamir mountains.

After the changes in the European cultural, intellectual and religious contexts during the eighteenth century under the influence of the Enlightenment, the problem of the location of the Garden of Eden was taken up in various secular disciplines. The outstanding Swedish botanist Carl von Linné (Linnaeus), for example, cited paradise as the source of the world's flora and fauna. He explained that the astonishing variety of the world's plants and animals was a result of their propagation from the primordial island of paradise and their dispersal, as the waters covering the rest of the globe gradually receded, to colonise the emerging land masses. In his *Treatise on*

Fig 92 *Albert R. Terry's map of the Garden of Eden and the four rivers, from his book* The Flood and Garden of Eden: Astounding Facts and Prophecies *(Elms Court, [Ilfracombe, Devon]: Arthur H. Stockwell, 1962; repr. 1963), p.12. London, British Library, 311.cc.44.*

the Origin of Language (1772), German writer and thinker Johann Gottfried Herder discussed the origin of languages in India and, as had almost every scholar before the Renaissance, saw the Ganges as one of the rivers of paradise.

More generally, in the course of the eighteenth century the traditional theological way of thinking about the Garden of Eden as the home of the first man and woman, Adam and Eve, was transformed in academic circles into a scientific search for the origin of humankind. In this form the question has involved mainstream scholars as well as those on the fringe. Of course, the concept of the original site of humankind is not the same as the idea of paradise. Comparative philologists, mythologists and archaeological ethnographers were not searching for the delightful place of the biblical paradise, but for the cradle of humankind. Their solutions – many including maps in support of their ideas – ranged from Greenland to Central Africa and from America to Central Asia. The favoured hypothesis was that the original birthplace of mankind was in Central Asia, either on the high plateau of the Pamirs or in Lemuria, a now submerged prehistoric continent below the northern Indian Ocean. The problem of accounting for the arrival of human beings in the Americas led to the idea of a 'Lost Atlantis' – a former land connection between the eastern and western hemispheres, of which the archipelagos of the Canaries, Madeira and the Azores may be relics. Maps were compiled by nineteenth-century scholars to demonstrate the progressive dispersion of the human race over the globe according to these theories.

As the nations of Europe began to colonise the New World, especially in the eighteenth century, their encounters with indigenous peoples were liable to be coloured by their ideas about paradise. For Denis Diderot, French philosopher and writer during the Enlightenment, for example, the simplicity of the languages and the 'natural' way of life of native Tahitians appeared 'close to the origin of the world'. The idea of paradise inspired the creation of botanical gardens for didactic purposes and for the study of natural history. Identifying the former site of paradise could provide an opportunity for promoting nationalism, as in the case of Franz von Wendrin. He claimed, not long after the First World War, that the earthly paradise was formerly in eastern Germany on the Mecklenburg-Pomeranian boundary at Demmin and that the Germans had driven the Jews out of paradise. The idea of paradise was also invoked in the context of palaeontological discoveries of early man. Some 500 years after fifteenth-century theologians had located paradise in Africa, the origin of the earliest hominids has been placed in eastern Africa, in Kenya and Ethiopia.

Such nineteenth- and twentieth-century enquiries about the original cradle of the ancestors of the human race, however, were no longer based on a sacred text, with all the difficulties, inevitable uncertainty and mystery that surrounds a God-given account. The modern plotting of the precise original site of humankind had to be based on scientific proof and direct observation, with no recourse to mythology or religion and no speculation about a 'paradise' or garden of any kind. Nevertheless, as William Fairfield Warren noted in 1885, the 'mother–region' of the human race proved to be 'as elusive and Protean as are any of the terrestrial Edens of theology, or of legend, or of poetry'.

Visual Interlude
Paradise in the Seychelles

◆

Charles George Gordon was a nineteenth-century English general, a hero of the British empire. He had fought in Crimea and eastern China before being chosen, in 1877, to be Governor-General of the equatorial provinces of Egypt (Fig 93). Also known as Gordon Pasha or General Chinese Gordon, he fought in Africa against the slave trade, went up the course of the River Nile and waged war against the insurgents in Sudan. In 1885, when Khartoum was besieged, he resisted for ten months. It was an ill-fated heroism, though. Only two days before reinforcements came, Khartoum fell and Gordon was killed.

Photo. by London Stereoscopic Company, Ltd.

GENERAL GORDON

Gordon Pasha took a keen interest in sacred history, and in 1881 he claimed to have discovered the site of the lost Garden of Eden on Praslin, the largest island of the Seychelles, the tiny but exquisite archipelago in the middle of the Indian Ocean. Gordon's preference for these islands was not only because they were full of delights. Praslin was the only place on earth where the palm tree known as *coco de mer* or *Lodoicea Seychellarum* grew. This tree has a male and female variant. The male flower clusters are phallus-shaped while the female flowers are the largest of any palm. The fruit, a double coconut, suggests the female pudenda, resembling, in Gordon's words, 'a belly with thighs' (Fig 94). In his view, this was formerly the forbidden fruit of the Tree of Knowledge of Good and Evil. From the view point of standard Christian doctrine, Gordon was wrong in associating sexuality

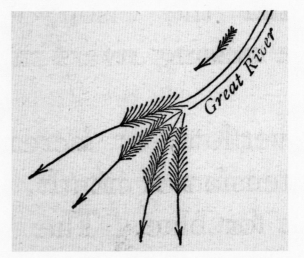

with original sin, which actually was the result of an act of pride, yet he was certain of his finding. He also identified on the island of Praslin the former Tree of Life – the bread-fruit palm known as *Artocarpus incisa*. Gordon acknowledged that these trees were now normal plants, but speculated that before the Fall they had been the Tree of Knowledge of Good and Evil and the Tree of Life mentioned in the Book of Genesis.

Gordon declared the local climate matched the description of an agreeably temperate paradise, and the three-foot long snakes that abounded on the island were, in his view, other relics of the Genesis narrative. He illustrated his theory with a map, included in the biography written after Gordon's death by his brother Henry William. The map, together with two marginal

diagrams, also show how the four streams described in Genesis ran *into* the river of paradise and not, as was usually thought, out of it (Figs 95 and 96). Thus instead of a single river flowing from Eden to water the garden, which then branched into four (the medieval idea) or divided outside paradise, both upstream and downstream, into two branches (Calvin's concept), Gordon saw four streams – those of the Gihon (which had become a dessicated course south of Jerusalem), the Nile (identified by Gordon as the Pison), the Tigris and the Euphrates – flowing into one river to water, further south, the garden. Before the Flood, he believed, Eden had spread over a huge region now covered by the Indian Ocean.

Fig 93 (opposite, below) *Portrait of Charles G. Gordon, from Lytton Strachey,* Eminent Victorians *(London: Chatto & Windus, 1918) p.217. London, British Library, 010803.g.11.*

Fig 94 (opposite, above) *Nut from the* coco de mer *in the Seychelles* (Lodoicea Seychellarum).

Fig 95 (above left) *The first of Charles G. Gordon's marginal diagrams of* The Four Rivers and the Great River, *from Henry William Gordon,* Events in the Life of Charles George Gordon, from its Beginning to its End *(London: Kegan Paul Trench, 1886), p.262. British Library, 32406.f.11.*

Fig 96 (above right) *The second of Charles G. Gordon's marginal diagrams of* The Four Rivers and the Great River.

Bibliographic Essay

◆

The tale of the prince eager to know about Eden is mentioned and commented upon by William F. Warren, *Paradise Found. The Cradle of the Human Race at the North Pole* (Boston: Houghton, Mifflin, 1885), p.XII. The quotation at the end of this chapter comes from p.43.

A useful survey of the discussion about Eden after the Enlightenment is found in Charles W. J. Withers, 'Geography, Enlightenment, and the Paradise Question', in David N. Livingstone and Charles W. J. Withers, eds., *Geography and Enlightenment* (Chicago–London: The University of Chicago Press, 1999), pp.67–92. The reader may recognise the declining interest in the geography of paradise on the part of mainstream biblical exegetes in the nineteenth century by looking at the entry on 'Eden' in William Smith, *Dictionary of the Bible*: *Comprising Its Antiquities, Biogeography, Geography, and Natural History*, 3 vols (London: John Murray, 1863), where the problem of the location of the Garden of Eden was abandoned as insoluble.

There is a vast literature on Old Testament criticism. A summary of the issues involved is found in Raymond E. Brown, Joseph A. Fitzmeyer, and Roland E. Murphy, eds., *The New Jerome Biblical Commentary* (Englewood Cliffs, NJ: Geoffrey Chapman, 1968, 1990), pp.3–13, 1146–65.

The arguments of the Assyriologists mentioned in this chapter are found in Austen Henry Layard, *Nineveh and Its Remains*, 2 vols (London: John Murray, 1849), II, p.472; Friedrich Delitzsch, *Babel and Bible. A Lecture on the Significance of Assyriological Research for Religion Delivered Before the German Emperor*, Thomas J. McCormack, trans. (Chicago: The Open Court Publishing Company, 1902); Friedrich Delitzsch, *Wo lag das Paradies?* (Leipzig: J.C. Hinrich, 1881); Friedrich Delitzsch, 'The "Babel/Bible" Controversy and Its Aftermath', in

Jack M. Sasson, ed., *Civilizations of the Ancient Near East*, 3 vols (New York: Charles Scribner's Sons, 1995), I, pp.95–106; Archibald Henry Sayce, *The Religions of Ancient Egypt and Babylonia. The Gifford Lectures on the Ancient Egyptian and Babylonian Conception of the Divine. Delivered in Aberdeen* (Edinburgh: T. and T. Clark, 1902), p.385; Sayce, *The Hibbert Lectures, 1887. Lectures on the Origin and Growth of Religion as Illustrated by the Religion of the Ancient Babylonians* (London: Williams and Norgate, 1887), pp.238–42; Sayce, *Fresh Light from the Ancient Monuments: A Sketch of the Most Striking Confirmations of the Bible from Recent Discoveries in Egypt, Assyria, Palestine, Babylonia, Asia Minor* (London: [n. publ.], 1883); William Willcocks, *From the Garden of Eden to the Crossing of the Jordan* (Cairo: The French Institute of Oriental Archaeology, 1918; 2nd edn, London: E and F. N. Spon Ltd., 1919, with imprint added in the margin); Manfred Dietrich, 'Das biblische Paradies und der babylonische Tempelgarten. Überlegungen zur Lage des Gartens Eden', in Bernd Janowski, Beate Ego and Annette Krüger, eds., *Das biblische Weltbild und seine altorientalischen Kontexte* (Tübingen: Mohr Siebeck, 2001), pp.280–323; Manfred Dietrich, 'Der "Garten Eden" und die babylonischen Parkanlagen im Tempelbezirk', in Johannes Hahn and Christian Ronning, eds., *Religiöse Landschaften* (Münster in Westphalia: Ugarit Verlag, 2002), pp.1–29.

For a general discussion of the developments of Assyrian studies in the nineteenth and twentieth centuries see the historiographic study in Mariana Giovino, *The Assyrian Sacred Tree: A History of Interpretations* (Fribourg-Göttingen: Academic Press-Vandenhoeck and Ruprecht, 2007), and Mogens Trolle Larsen, 'Seeing Mesopotamia', in Ann C. Gunter, ed., *The Construction of the Ancient Near East, Culture and History*, 11 (1992), pp.126–8.

See also Brook Wilensky-Lanford, *Paradise Lust: Searching for the Garden of Eden* (New York: Grove Press, 2011), pp.24–47; 65–83; 100–18.

Other books, maps and authors discussed in the chapter include: *From Paradise Lost to Paradise Regained* (Brooklyn, NY: Watchtower Bible and Tract Society of New York, 1958) [Jehovah's Witnesses]; Moritz Engel, *Die Lösung der Paradiesfrage* (Leipzig: Otto Schulze, 1885); A. P. Curtis, *The Land of Eden and Havilah* (London: the author, 1905); Albert Herrmann, *Die Erdkarte der Urbibel* (Braunschweig: Kommissionsverlag von Georg Westermann, 1931); Kamal Salibi, *The Bible Came from Arabia* (London: Jonathan Cope, 1996); Richard Hennig, *Wo lag das Paradies* (Berlin: Ullstein Verlag, 1950); Lars Ivar Ringbom, *Paradisus terrestris: myt, bild och verklighet* (Copenhagen–Helsinki: Ejnar Munksgaards–Akademiska Bokhandeln–Nordiska Antikvariska Bokhandeln, 1958); David Rohl, *Legend, the Genesis of Civilisation* (London: Century, 1998), pp.46–68; James E. Nicholson, *The Probable "Garden of Eden": A Long-Forgotten Star Myth* (London: Watts, 1935, for private circulation only); Albert R. Terry, *The Flood and Garden of Eden: Astounding Facts and Prophecies* (Elms Court, Ilfracombe, Devon: Arthur H. Stockwell, 1962; repr.1963); Chris Ward, http://www.logoschristian. org/triangle.html; Emilio Spedicato, 'Eden Revisited: Geography, Numerics and Other Tales', *Report DMSIA, Miscellanea* 1/01 (2001), version revised in 2003; 'Geography and Numerics of Eden, Kharsag and Paradise: Sumerian and Enochian Sources versus the Genesis Tale', http://itis.volta. alessandria.it/episteme/ep7/ep7-eden.htm; Carl von Linné, *Oratio de telluris habitabilis incremento* (Leiden: Cornelius Haak, 1744); Johann Herder, *Abhandlung über den Ursprung der Sprache* (Berlin: Voss, 1772); Denis Diderot, *Supplément au Voyage de Bougainville*, Herbert Dieckmann, ed. (Geneva-Lille: Droz-Giard, 1955); Friedrich von Wendrin, *Die Entdeckung des Paradies* (Leipzig: Braunschweig, 1924). An overview of nineteenth-century secular theories locating the cradle of human civilisation is found in Warren, *Paradise Found* (1885), pp.33–43.

Fred Plaut has studied Gordon's theories and map about Eden, in *Analysis Analysed. When the Map Becomes the Territory* (London–New York: Routledge, 1993), pp.145–72, where Gordon's ideas are analysed from a psychological point of view. Gordon's arguments and map about Eden are published in Henry William Gordon, *Events in the Life of Charles George Gordon, from its Beginning to its End* (London: Kegan Paul Trench, 1886), pp.261–9.

Fig 97 Paradise in the Middle East, *according to the Jehovah's Witnesses's publication* From Paradise Lost to Paradise Regained *(Brooklyn, NY: Watchtower Bible and Tract Society of New York, 1958), endpapers. Detail: the Fall, the Expulsion and other biblical events.*

CHAPTER 9

PARADISE AND UTOPIA

Imagine there's no heaven,
It's easy if you try
No hell below us
Above us only sky
Imagine all the people
Living for today...
Imagine there's no countries
It isn't hard to do
Nothing to kill or die for
And no religion too
Imagine all the people
Living life in peace...
Imagine no possessions
I wonder if you can
No need for greed or hunger
A brotherhood of man
Imagine all the people
Sharing all the world...
You may say I'm a dreamer
But I'm not the only one
I hope some day you'll join us
And the world will be as one

JOHN LENNON,
IMAGINE, 1971

Visual Closure

◆

MAPS OF UTOPIA

Louvain, December 1516. A work of fiction describing a perfect human society has just been published. It is a *libellus* or 'booklet', written in Latin, that represents the product of a network of like-minded printers and intellectuals. The publisher is Thierry Martens, a humanist printer with a successful and widespread business; the editors are Desiderius Erasmus of Rotterdam, a priest who is also an excellent classical scholar and theologian, and Peter Gilles, a senior administrative officer of the city of Antwerp. The title of this new work is *Utopia*, a word coined by the author, Thomas More,

an English lawyer with a bent for the humanities.

More turns to the imagination to describe a perfect island society in a place located, as the title of his work suggests, 'nowhere'. More's invention of the composite term *Utopia* (literally, 'no place') is derived from the Greek words *ou* ('not') and *topos* ('place'). Within the book, however, the reader finds a poem headed *Six lines on the island of Utopia*, in which More claims that the correct name for that self-contained, perfect universe should be not *Utopia*, but *Eutopia*, from the Greek *eu* ('good') plus *topos* ('place'). More, in short, is imagining a place that is simultaneously both a 'no place' and a 'good place' – a happy commonwealth located nowhere.

Fig 99 (left) *Hans Holbein,* Sir Thomas More, *England, 1527. New York, The Frick Collection.*

This paradoxical idea is found in visions of perfection throughout the world and all over the ages: the perfect human society that exists somewhere and that is located nowhere. Such a notion has hovered in the background throughout our history of the mapping of paradise. Interestingly, Sir Thomas More (as he became in 1521) was a convinced believer in the literal meaning of the Book of Genesis and was critical of those allegorical readings of the Bible that questioned the continued existence of the earthly paradise. Following medieval tradition in this respect, he insisted that the original paradise of Adam and Eve had survived somewhere on earth, affirming that anyone who doubted the contemporary existence of the earthly Garden of Eden was to be considered 'a very heretike'.

Fig 98 (opposite and previous page, detail) *Ambrosius Holbein (attr.),* Map of the island of Utopia and the Alphabet of the Utopians, *from Thomas More,* Utopia *(Louvain: Thierry Martens, 1516), title woodcut and first page. London, British Library, C.27.b.30.*

More's booklet was an immediate success. As with the word 'paradise' all those millennia earlier, his neologism quickly entered Western languages, although with fewer permutations, and 'utopian' or 'utopistic' are now in daily use. The words refer to the attitude of those who *imagine* a society better than the one around them (as well as to the rich literary genre that developed from More's *libellus*). Of course, Thomas More was not the first, and John Lennon was neither the last nor the only one, to imagine and describe a vision of a radically new and perfect human condition.

At the beginning of this book we referred to the richness and universality of the human predisposition to imagine worlds other than the visible and tangible one. The long history of mapping paradise emphasises that in Western Christianity, in particular, a deep-seated tendency to conceive an earthly place of human perfection has always been present. More's *Utopia* tells the story of King Utopus's cutting through an isthmus to create an island. In its separateness, we can see Utopia as a parallel of paradise, separated from the ordinary world by its distance in space (represented by a geographical barrier such as an inaccessible mountain peak or an impassable ocean) and its remoteness in time (result of the Fall and the Flood). More also coined other words, such as the name of the river (*Anydris*, 'waterless') and the ruler (prince *Ademus*, 'without subjects'), all as ways of addressing the key question: how to conceive a state of human perfection that has a place in history and a location in the physical world while being outside time and space?

Nevertheless, again as with paradise, the elusiveness of More's Utopia did not prevent attempts to visualise it. The first edition of his book, published in Louvain in 1516, included a

Amanroti vrbs.

Fons Anydri.

Ostium anydri.

hythlodaeus.

woodcut portraying the island. The picture, which may have been the work of Ambrosius Holbein, Hans Holbein's elder brother, is called *Utopiae insulae figura*, a 'depiction of the island of Utopia' (Fig 98). The island has a large harbour, protected by a tower at the entrance, and three ships in the foreground. Inland, the course of the 'waterless river' forms a crescent as it flows from its source (*Fons Anydri*) to its mouth (*Ostium Anydri*) and passes through the capital city of Amaurot (in Greek, the 'shadowy' or 'unknown' place).

The second edition of the book (Paris, 1517) was not illustrated, but Ambrosius Holbein was almost certainly the artist responsible for the sophisticated picture that appeared in the third edition (Johann Froben, Basel, 1518) (Fig 100). The title is now slightly different, *Utopiae insulae tabula*, a 'map of the island of Utopia', and some details have been changed. For example, human figures stand in the foreground, two on the left and one on the right. One of those on the left, labelled Hythlodaeus, is pointing out the island to his companion, identified from More's narrative to be More himself. The figure on the right may represent Peter Gilles, clerk of the city of Utopia but also a real person, the editor of *Utopia*'s first edition.

The image is familiar. In 2005, however, new light was shed on its meaning when Malcolm Bishop published an article in the *British Dental Journal* in which he suggested that the 1518 image depicts not an island but a human skull (Fig 103). Bishop is a dentist, and it was his experience in dental radiology that led him first to perceive the ship's ribs and planking of the ship as a set of teeth, then to focus on the anatomical structure of the skull, and finally

Fig 100 *Ambrosius Holbein (attr.),* Map of the island of Utopia, *from Thomas More,* Utopia *(Basel: Johann Froben, 1518). London, British Library, G.2398, p.12.*

to recognise the entire image as a symbol of death. Bishop describes the lower row of rectangles on the ship's broadside as 'the bony root prominences of the lower incisors and premolars' and points to Hythlodaeus's back as outlining the back of a neck and the lighter figure of More as marking the spine. He interprets the land in the foreground as shoulders, the dark figure on the right as shaping the mandible, the main mast of the large ship as defining the nasal cavity and, finally, the hill that in this image replaces the harbour suggesting an eyebrow. The whole image, Bishop speculates, may have been the inspiration of Erasmus, the Renaissance humanist and theologian with whom Thomas More used to enjoy playing with words and drawing out their different meanings.

Seen in such light, Holbein's map is a visual pun. The image of death, which would have been widely recognised as evoking the Christian warning *memento mori* ('remember your mortality'), could also have been intended to say 'remember More' (*memento Mori*). Taking the argument further, Bishop suggests that by representing the act of imagining Utopia in a human skull, symbol of death, the artist is hinting that More's dream is the product of a mind destined to die. Bishop reads a yet more sinister significance from the image: a reminder that in More's day the holding of utopian ideals risked punishment by death. We may see an even wider message: that there is something potentially deadly associated with any utopian vision. Utopian projects to install a new and perfect political order have always had great appeal, as they express the desire to put an end to history and even remake the human condition. But what has been the outcome? Humanity's struggle to impose rigid order and strict control on the free flow of social life seem to be doomed to failure.

IMAGINE THERE'S NO EDEN

It is frequently remarked that a map displays the territory, but is not itself the territory, the point of Borges's short story mentioned in chapter 2. Maps represent the world, but in so doing they inevitably transform, simplify, distort it. Maps seek to trap a multi-dimensional and ever-changing reality in abstract graphic symbols. They may compress truth or hold hidden meanings. They certainly demand imaginative reading. Like any work of art, a map is a 'lie' that forces us to appreciate the truth, another commonplace in the history and theory of cartography. Just as in the first century BC Diodorus of Sicily, with whom we

started our voyage through this book, persisted in compiling his universal history while knowing full well that such a narrative is contrary to nature, so the mapmaker has to measure and classify as he aims at a clear definition, and discovers the limits of his abstraction.

We too, in this book, have made a conceptual journey, pursuing the elusive paradise, but our maps of the earthly paradise have guided our way from late antiquity and the beginnings of Christianity through the Middle Ages and the Renaissance to the present day. We have seen

Fig 101 *The dead Tree of Adam, from* The Times *of 23 December 1944.*

how the issues of locating the earthly paradise on a map was always related to contemporary Christian teaching about the ultimate destiny of human life. We have also appreciated that while modern attempts to map paradise may be viewed by modern mainstream theologians as the province of fringe and fundamentalist mavericks, in the past established theology took a very different approach. We have been reminded, in short, that those archaic ways of thinking are in fact an indissoluble component of our intellectual history.

As we look back at the journey we have taken in this book, we may reflect on what we have learnt from the enduring debate over the location of paradise. One conclusion is that the debate reveals more about the people involved than about the issue itself. Different situations and contexts offer different choices and approaches as scholarly thought is blown hither and thither by the winds of history. Irrespective of who has been involved – a medieval mapmaker, a Renaissance biblical scholar or a Middle or Near East archaeologist – the dynamic tension between symbolic and literal approaches seems to represent a fundamental polarity inherent in the human mind. Another conclusion, drawn especially from the maps, is that however the issue of the location of paradise on earth was moulded and remoulded by each generation, none of the 'last words' on the location of the Garden of Eden has ever been effectively final. Finally, and above all, it is clear that universal and profound human needs lie at the roots of all forms of the nostalgia for a lost or future paradise, or a utopian impulse. The human race longs to be united in safety and peace, for each individual to find a purpose that is higher than that defined by physical existence,

and to be spared violence, injustice and social alienation.

Sadly, though, the earthly paradise is not on *Google Earth*. No road map or satellite navigation database is capable of directing the hunt for such an elusive place, and dreams of better worlds have all too often turned into nightmares. The establishment of a truly perfect society on earth seems to be a chimera, just as the location of the unlocatable paradise has proved out of reach. We think of Apollo, the mythical Greek god. Apollo was in love with a beautiful nymph, Daphne, and was ready to pursue her to the ends of the earth. No sooner had he reached her, however, her arms sprouted the branches of a tree, her feet grew roots, her skin was turned into bark, her hair was transformed into leaves and she was metamorphosed into a laurel. Seized by love, the god could not seize the object of his desires; as he touched her, he found himself embracing a tree (Fig 102). Likewise, in seeking our paradise on earth, we too pursue a perfection that is in continuous flight away from us. We may dream of a better world, but it eludes our grasp, and an experience of a paradise or a utopia in time and space appears to be impossible.

We began this book with John Lennon's *Imagine*, in which he sang about his wish for a world without nations or religion, without wars or property and without heaven or hell. Lennon was dreaming of a world free from fear and conflicts. He was imagining global peace for all, the liberation of the human spirit from religions which divide and segregate, and hoping for a universal brotherhood in this world. But it is just a short step from universal brotherhood to a totalitarian society, where brothers and sisters find themselves compelled to be happy and forced

to be free. Lennon, of course, was seeking release rather than restriction; but taken literally his radical words announced a closed world where all the people 'that live for today' are locked inside. And yet, despite being a song in praise of a world without any other worlds, *Imagine* was a hymn to another world and not to the one that is around us.

The former Beatle and pacifist is not 'the only one' to have dreamed of better worlds. Thomas More, an example for all, imagined in the sixteenth century an ideal republic guided by virtue and reason, perfectly ordered for the common good. Nearly 20 years after the publication of his *Utopia*, St Thomas More (who had kept his Catholic faith in an age of violent upheaval and in a country ruled by a king in direct conflict with the Pope) was imprisoned in the Tower of London and executed. In very different circumstances and several centuries later on 8 December 1980, 9 years and 3 months after the release of *Imagine*, revolutionary pacifist John Lennon was shot dead outside his New York apartment. Both of these events, although historically and culturally separated from each other, nonetheless bring to mind a photograph, published in *The Times* towards the end of the

Second World War, of the dead Tree of Adam, which serves as an image of how violence can shatter nostalgia – whether real or imagined – of a better world (Fig 101). The article accompanying this illustration reported that the tree near to the confluence of the Tigris and the Euphrates (the Tree of Knowledge from the Garden of Eden, according to local tradition) had died. In the course of another conflict, the invasion of Iraq in 2003, the Western media reported that this site was a desolate wasteland of cracked paving stones and bullet holes, and that Adam's Tree was dead. Nostalgia for paradise always intensifies in times of strife.

Despite all kinds of trouble and violence, people everywhere have shared a yearning for the full joy of a real paradise. Thomas More and John Lennon, along with all of us, try to escape from a world without other worlds, and break through the sky above in search of some kind of heaven, even at the risk of succumbing to totalitarian tendencies. After all, a concept of history which does not allow for other temporal modalities, and a concept of geography which lacks blessed islands, black holes and enchanted mountains, quickly becomes very limited indeed.

Fig 102 *Antonio del Pollaiuolo,* Apollo and Daphne, *Florence, c.1470–80. London, National Gallery.*

Bibliographic Essay

◆

Thomas More's *Utopia* was first published in Louvain by Thierry Martens in 1516. The second edition was printed in Paris by Gilles de Gourmont in 1517 and the third in Basel by Johann Froben in 1518. The full title of Thomas More's fiction on a perfect, self-contained society is *Libellus vere aureus, nec minus salutaris quam festivus, de optimo rei publicae statu deque nova insula Utopia*. In the English translation published by Ralph Robinson in 1551 and 1556 the title is rendered as *A Fruteful and Pleasant Worke of the Beste State of a Publique Weale, and of the newe yle called Utopia*. I have made use of Thomas More, *Utopia*, George M. Logan, Robert M. Adams and Clarence H. Miller, eds (Cambridge: Cambridge University Press, 1995).

The literature on More's *Utopia* is, of course, vast. Here mention can be made of George M. Logan, *The Meaning of More's Utopia* (Princeton: Princeton University Press, 1983) and Quentin Skinner, 'Sir Thomas More's *Utopia* and the Language of Renaissance Humanism', in Anthony Pagden, ed., *Ideas in Context: The Languages of Political Theory in Early-Modern Europe* (Cambridge: Cambridge University Press, 1987), pp.123–57. Malcolm Bishop presented his theory about the skull hidden in the 1518 map of Utopia in 'Ambrosius Holbein's *memento mori* Map for Sir Thomas More's *Utopia*: The Meanings of a Masterpiece of Early Sixteenth Century Graphic Art', *British Dental Journal*, 199/2 (July 2005), pp.107–12.

Fig 103 (above) *Enhanced image of Ambrosius Holbein, Map of the island of Utopia, 1518, from Malcolm Bishop, 'Ambrosius Holbein's* memento mori Map for Sir Thomas More's Utopia: The Meanings of a Masterpiece of Early Sixteenth-Century Graphic Art', *British Dental Journal, 199/2 (July 2005), p.111.*

Fig 104 (opposite) *Map of the world from Ranulf Higden's* Polychronicon, *Ramsey, England, c. 1350. British Library, Royal ms 14.c.IX; fols 1v–2r. The large rectangle at the top of the map has been left blank, presumably in anticipation of a specialist illuminator who would have drawn Adam and Eve in paradise.*

Index

Picture Credits

Air Mauritius: 1; Album/Oronoz/akg-images:.25; Akademie Verlag, Berlin: p.53, 47, 48, 49; Courtesy Malcolm Bishop: 103; Parker Library, Corpus Christi College, Cambridge: 28; Courtesy of *COLORS* magazine: 12; Didier Descouens: 94; The John and Mable Ringling Museum of Art, the State Art Museum of Florida: 5, 6; The Mappa Mundi Trust, Hereford: 31, 34, 35, 36, 37, 39, 40, 41, 42, 43; Dr Albert Knoepfli Stiftung: 53; National Museums of Liverpool/Bridgeman Art Library: 4; British Library, London: p.1, p.7, 7, 8, 9, 10, 11, p.37, 23, 27, 29, 33, 45, 46, 50, 51, 52, 54, p.99, 62, 63, 64, 65, 66, 67, 68, p.117, 69, 70, 71, 72, 73, 74, 75, 76, 77, 78, 79, 80, 81, 82, 83, 84, 85, p.143, 86, 87, 89, 90, 91, 92, 93, 95, 96, 98, 100, 101; British Museum, London: 2, 3; College of Arms, London: 30; The National Gallery, London/akg-images: 102; Bibliothèque Municipale, Mâcon: 13, 14; Biblioteca Estense, Modena: p.2, 56, 57; The Frick Collection, New York: 99; Biblioteca Nazionale Universitaria, Turin: 26; Biblioteca Apostolica Vaticana: 17, 18, 19, 20, 21, 22, 24, 55; Biblioteca Nazionale Marciana, Venice: p.79, 59, 58, 60; Biblioteca Civica, Verona: 15, 16; Herzog August Bibliothek, Wolfenbüttel: 44.

Antiochia.

Edeßa

MESOPOTAMI

Hierapolis.

Charre olim
Charan

Singaras mons

Nicephorium

Reschipha olim
Retseph.

Pacoria
Olim
Pethor.

OCCIDENZ

SIRIE PARS

Euphrates fl.

Agaman

Sabe

CH

Montana Arab Felicis

ARA
BIA

Montana Chaldae

DESERTA.